ORAL:
The warm, intimate, unauthorized portrait of a Man of God

ORAL:
The warm, intimate, unauthorized portrait of a Man of God

Wayne A. Robinson

Acton House, Inc.
Publishers

Los Angeles, California

Copyright © 1976 by Acton House, Inc.

All rights reserved. No part of this book may be reproduced or utilized in any form or by any means, electronic or mechanical, including photocopying, recording, or by any information storage and retrieval system, without permission in writing from the Publisher. Inquiries should be addressed to Acton House, Inc., Publishers, 1888 Century Park East, Suite 216, Los Angeles, California 90067.

ISBN 0-89202-003-2

Printed in the United States of America

Dedication

To those special people in the Oral Roberts organizations, many who've moved on, including Bill Armstrong, from whom I learned the most; Al Bush, manager *par excellence* of people, money and programs; Ruth Rooks, Oral's secretary *extraordinaire;* Carl Hamilton, cousin, predecessor and colleague; as well as Bob DeWeese, Leon Hartz, Collins Steele, Bob Brooks, Mary Bea May, Marion Collins, Tommy Tyson, George Stovall, and many more.

Table of Contents

Preface

IN WRITING this book one of the surprising problems was to determine what name I would use for Oral Roberts. He's addressed in many ways: Mister Roberts, Brother Roberts, Reverend Roberts, Dr. Roberts, President Roberts, Rev, O. R., Oral. Journalists refer to him in their stories as Roberts. I decided finally to use the one he asked me to use several years ago.

It was during my first summer-time employment with the Oral Roberts Association, while still a graduate student at SMU. Bill Armstrong, managing editor of *Abundant Life Magazine,* asked me to accompany him for a presentation of the next issue. It was to be only my second direct encounter with the famous evangelist, and on the way to ORU, I pondered how I should address him. I didn't like "Brother Roberts" and I felt uncomfortable with "President Roberts." The question remained unresolved as I entered the conference room and I heard myself addressing him as "Mister Roberts." That didn't seem right either and I started to change it, but in a warm fashion he said, "Call me 'Oral,' Wayne." "Oral" it was, and Oral it has been in the years since.

Oral is a gifted, driven, complex man. At times he has been a joy to work with, and at other times he created in me a devastating insecurity. In the description of Bob DeWeese, a former longtime associate, he can either put his best foot forward or do exactly the opposite.

My opinion is that the phenomenon which he represents somehow fulfills the desires of millions of people. Most people want to believe there are special persons who have the key, who know the incantation, that will release the power of God into their lives. The wish produces a climate in which people like Jean Dixon, the late Kathryn Kuhlman, Oral Roberts, Billy Graham and their thousands of imitators can flourish with incredible success. Oral particularly satisfies a deep psychic hunger in untold numbers of people; he eases their sense of alienation from an unfriendly world and assuages their fears of a universe turned hostile. Only with this ability can a once obscure and ridiculed sawdust-trail preacher command a television audience of 50 million: he is phenomenally attuned to what people want and need to hear and is particularly endowed to deliver answers to those needs.

This book does not address the question of how people have come to want the sort of attention that Oral gives them; rather, it focuses on what he does and how and—to the extent possible—why. Neither is this the definitive, much less authorized, biography. Its rationale arises out of my own feelings about, and insights into, a really incredible human being.

In many instances, I am examining the interface between Oral Roberts and Wayne Robinson, and on occasion that inward look has proved painful. Yet this is a book I have felt the urge to write for many years. Moreover, it needed to be written. Strange as it may seem, only one book about Oral Roberts has ever been published, and it is his autobiography, *The Call*, which necessarily has limited perspective and is dated, having been written during early 1971.

Some will charge that I was so close to the forest I couldn't see the trees; others will say that the book is a hatchet job, born of resentment. Oral himself probably won't read it at all, judging by past performance. He declined to read my earlier book, *I Once Spoke in Tongues*, which contained four minor references to him, all affirming. He told his secretary, Ruth Rooks, "I think too much of Wayne to read it. I don't want my opinion of him to change." And Ruth herself wondered aloud why I chose to write that book on that topic at that time.

I'm convinced that trying to please other people is an inadequate reason for a book. I don't have a great need to bare my soul or to disassociate myself from a part of my past. I simply feel here's a story that adds a needed dimension to understanding one part of American religious life.

This, then, is not a negative study. Oral is already one of the most criticized of religious leaders. Despite his critics' best, thousands turn to him every day for prayer and counsel. And, as I have stated, it is not a definitive study. It does not pretend to objectivity. Instead, I have striven for balance, honesty, and fairness.

Above all, I have attempted to reveal the human dimensions of Oral Roberts—which his millions of followers and anti-followers cannot possibly see when their view is blocked by all the gleaming trappings and gold-colored buildings, and circumscribed by a television frame.

Here then is "Oral," who, at different times in the recent past, has been friend, employer, and co-worker.

Wayne A. Robinson
June, 1976

CHAPTER 1

The Secret That Explains His Success

UPON RECEIVING my first paycheck from the Oral Roberts Evangelistic Association, Inc., I drove into downtown Tulsa to buy a new suit. In seminary I hadn't worried about clothes, but student dress hardly seemed appropriate in the six-story, mid-city marble building that housed the international headquarters of the Reverend Oral Roberts. Until the late fifties, white pants and wild-colored coats had been "in," but a New York public relations firm on a $100,000 retainer stopped that. Now, during coffee breaks the cafeteria resembled the board room of a conservative bank; a good black suit was a priority.

On the recommendation of a cousin, I went to Clarke's. The salesman who greeted me and began showing me a rack of suits was fluent in profanity. It wasn't that he was angry; it was simply his medium for conversing. Virtually every sentence was laced with some descriptive four-letter word or off-color phrase. This didn't really bother me—my concern was to select a suit, which I did. The salesman escorted me onto the elevator and, as we rode down to the cashier's office, he asked where I worked. When I told him I was employed by Oral Roberts, he was visibly shaken. He seemed unsure whether or not he should apologize for his four-letter language and the jokes. Instead, he said brightly, "You'll really like this suit; it'll be great for praying!"

I was flabbergasted. A minute earlier he had been an expert on profanity; now he was an authority on suits for praying. More incredible, I thought, was his notion that working for Oral Roberts was synonymous with praying. One of the first realizations of the successful employee at the old Oral Roberts Evangelistic Association (the "Evangelistic" was dropped in 1969) was that although people identified your job with prayer, it was in fact part of a business and a highly successful one at that.

Consider the present situation. At last count there were six foreign offices—in Great Britain, Canada, South Africa, India, Australia and New Zealand. There is Oral Roberts University (ORU), with a faculty and staff of four hundred; the Oral Roberts Association, with five hundred employees; and the University Village, a retirement center employing a hundred. He has a weekly radio and television show, plus a quarterly prime-time special broadcast over a hook-up larger than any two of the national networks combined. The Abundant Life Prayer Group, staffed by full-time prayer counselors twenty-four hours a day, receives over 200,000 long-distance calls a year. A media center at ORU is a top tourist attraction in Tulsa. Annually the Roberts enterprises mail more than one hundred and fifty million printed pieces over the world; magazines, books, tracts and tapes are dispatched by the thousands daily. There's even an in-house advertising agency.

Computers of the latest design provide instant information retrieval on all facets of the operations. A personnel office processes applicants and administers employee programs. Certified public accountants oversee the treasury and accounting divisions, while investment and endowment specialists, along with field representatives, staff a growing development office. Lawyers draft agreements, artists design visual materials, writers prepare articles. Vice presidents, division chiefs, department heads, administrative assistants, supervisors, management trainees, secretaries, clerks, typists, janitors, cafeteria workers, security guards—all fill their niches. Yet, Mr. and Mrs. Joe Jones in Typical City, U.S.A., have an image of Oral Roberts surrounded by helpers whose specialty is praying—and who need suits appropriate to this activity.

When you work for Oral Roberts you'd better be able to do more than pray if you hope to stay. If you must pray, do it on your own time, not his, and only after you've completed the work you brought home with you. The only prayers that count are those of one man, Oral Roberts.

People ask me, "What kind of man is he?" They also want to know about money matters, healing, basketball, ORU, or some statement he's made. But most often, they want to know what makes him tick.

Understanding Oral Roberts is a twenty-four-hour task and an impossible one. One management consultant who for ninety days observed the Tulsa operations reported that the executive staff spent eighty percent of their time "Oral gazing"—that is, trying to anticipate and decipher Oral's attitudes and wishes.

The one most important key to Oral Roberts' achievements is his incredible power as a *motivator*. Sick persons are motivated to believe they can be healed; businessmen are motivated to believe they can succeed; students are motivated to seek high grades; and his staff is motivated to perform at a level they never dreamed possible. These motivated people gladly testify to their successes. The sick or depressed witness that they've found health and happiness; others proclaim that they were broke financially and the ministry of Oral Roberts turned their situations around.

But there's a principle at work that's often missed by the casual observer: not only do people want to be as he says they can become; they also want to do it *for Oral*. If they're in a wheelchair they desperately want to walk, yes—but they also want *to please Oral*.

Illustration: A crusade in 1966 in the Midwest. Publicity and advance promotions assure crowds in the thousands. For weeks previous the crusade advance team has met with the sponsoring pastors. From their churches prayer counselors have been selected with weekly training sessions now in progress. One week before opening, a fleet of sleek tandem trucks pulls onto the state fairgrounds. Collins Steele, Crusade Manager, soon has the world's largest tent—one-quarter mile in circumference!—going up. Chairs are carefully placed to insure a full house on opening night. Sawdust is spread. Lights are erected. A platform, with a place for an organ and piano, is constructed. In back of it is a small booth in which Oral will meditate and await his part in the service. Collins will personally secure the hot water and a strong squeeze of lemon juice Oral will require between his sermon and praying for the sick. During the crusade as the weekend approaches a huge television crew from New York will fly in with scorching lights, miles of wiring, cameras and consoles, but for now the attention is focused on preparing for the Tuesday afternoon opening service, when Crusade Director and Associate Evangelist, the Reverend Robert F. DeWeese, will be speaking.

Bob DeWeese has been with Oral since 1950. A former pastor, swimming champion, and airplane pilot he knows better than anyone else close to Oral what a working relationship with Oral demands. He never tries to preach better than Oral nor does he ever do a poor job. He's the perfect team man, ready to fade into the shadows when necessary and capable of stepping into the limelight if required.

When Tuesday afternoon arrives, several thousand people from across this state and surrounding states have come. The service is low key and informal. Bob carefully orchestrates a mixture of information and inspiration. When there is a need for ushers or persons to distribute books, cards or pamphlets, Collins Steele stands on the sideline sending in small or large teams of volunteers to fulfill the assigned task.

After the singing and offering, and before the sermon, Bob moves to the topic for which most people have come: how to be prayed for or how to have a friend or loved one prayed for.

First, he shows them the book, If You Need Healing Do These Things. *"Brother Roberts wants everyone who will be in the prayer line to have a copy of this book and to have read at least the first four chapters. In a moment ushers will be passing through the audience to wait upon you. The cost of the book is only $1; if you cannot afford it, please take one free as a gift from Brother Roberts. Ushers, please wait upon the audience."*

Next, he holds up a card,—'a prayer card'—which asks for name, address, and brief description of the illness. And most important: a statement to be signed granting permission to be televised, photographed and recorded, as well as releasing the Oral Roberts Association and Oral personally from any liabilities incurred as a result of his prayers. In the upper right-hand corner different letters of the alphabet appear. Though the recipients are not aware of it, these letters determine who is prayed for on what nights. The first night there will be no more than 100 permitted, but by the last day the line may stretch double file around the entire tent. Bob also explains that for those who are unable to stand in the prayer line there is a special invalid's tent nearby where they can listen to a broadcast of the whole service, after which Oral will personally pray for each one. The afternoon service also gives Collins time to check out any problems with the sound and lighting system.

Soon the afternoon service is over, prayer cards have been distributed, and the sick and the dying, their friends and relatives, the curiosity seekers, and the faithful religious begin to fill the thousands of metal chairs. At 7:00 the organist and pianist begin to play. Before long the first main service of the crusade is ready to begin. Vep Ellis, song writer, soloist, and music director, leads the audience of six to seven thousand in hymns and choruses. Around 8 p.m. Bob learns that Oral has arrived and he introduces him immediately. But instead of preaching, Oral spends a few moments welcoming the audience, acknowledging the presence of dignitaries, and putting his audience at ease. Photographer's cameras click often . . . no flash cameras once the sermon starts. If his voice is husky, he has everyone stand to sing, "Amazing Grace." The tape track will reveal later that throughout the song he will clear his voice several times, sing a few words, and clear it again. After the song, a few more words and when he feels the rapport is there, he introduces Vep to sing a solo. It's Vep's task to set the mood for the sermon, which he does exceedingly well. As soon as he finishes, Bob steps forward to make the formal introduction of Oral which always ends on cue with the words, "And now the man that God has raised up with a message of healing for this generation, Oral Roberts!"

There is a great deal of applause. As it subsides, Oral asks everyone to stand for the reading of scripture. Though for many years he was hesitant to do so, he now puts on his glasses as he prepares to read. Then comes his prayer, followed by "Thank you and be seated please."

In the early days of the crusades, Oral was a spellbinder with sermons sometimes exceeding two hours in length. His love of the language and command of rhetoric and persuasion were such that he could move people emotionally, by preaching, as few could. (Dr. Joseph Quillian, dean of SMU's Perkins School of Theology, told Oral, in my presence, that one Sunday morning while his wife was in the hospital he was at home mopping the kitchen floor. He was paying no particular attention to the radio which was playing when suddenly he realized that a voice had broken into his reverie, seizing him with its beauty and feeling.

"Oral, it was you preaching and when you were through, I wanted to stand with mop in my hand and sing the Te Deum.*")*

But, as the middle years approached, and because of the emotional stress created by the ever-lengthening prayer line which followed his sermons, he trimmed his sermons both in length and intensity. Their sometimes conversational style contrasted sharply with the early-day fire.

At the close of his sermon, an invitation is given for those who want to commit their lives to Christ.

"Take the first step and slip up your hand . . . and hands are going up all over the place . . . Amen and God bless you for that. Now I want you to take the second step and stand to your feet. That's right, stand up, right where you are. And they're getting up . . . Please keep standing. Now, I want to pray for you and all the others that have stood. So please take the next step and join me here at the front for my prayer as Vep Ellis comes now to sing."

Immediately, the prayer counselors begin to leave their seats joining themselves to each one who comes. As with the Billy Graham Crusades, it's not unusual that half of those who come forward are trained prayer counselors, who will attempt to insure that the ones who have come also will go later to the prayer tent outside for additional prayer, counsel and the forms to be filled out for further information and study courses.

Oral welcomes the ones who have come. Photographers have

already taken the pictures and now he has the congregation stand to join in praying the "Sinner's Prayer." He finishes and announces that he will be back in a moment to pray for the sick. Bob DeWeese introduces one of the sponsoring pastors who welcomes those who've come forward and also invites them to one of their churches.

While that's taking place, Oral steps to the back of the platform, quickly exits, with Collins Steele on one side and another assistant on the other, and marches to the invalid tent—stopping for no one. The invalid tent is sometimes a microcosm of the worst illnesses and diseases. Water babies, retardates, the deformed and crippled, wasted skeletons on stretchers attended by nurses with oxygen and intravenous tubes, these are mixed with dozens of wheelchairs, mothers, fathers, sons and daughters awaiting expectantly, hopefully and desperately. With each one, he pauses, reads the card, says a prayer and moves on. Cameras click and interviews follow.

Back in the big tent, meanwhile, a prayer line is forming. Oral returns to the bigtop and stops in the booth back of the platform for his hot water with lemon juice. After a minute or two of concentration—athletes would say he was "psyching" himself—he bounds onto the platform, smiling and emanating warmth, compassion and sincerity.

Unfortunately for Oral, the first night of this crusade the very first person in the prayer line is a blind woman. Seldom do blind people claim to be helped by Oral's prayers and in meetings with small groups of friendly pastors, he himself acknowledges this reality. Still, he never refuses to pray for them, in spite of the tough sledding that he knows he faces. And, he never tries to manipulate them to the back of the line.

On this night he follows his usual practice of sharing several minutes with those at the head of the line so as to "build the faith of the people." He talks to the blind woman about her problem. Facing her, he places his left hand on the back of her head, his right hand over her eyes. He prays for fifteen or twenty seconds, then pauses.

"What's happening inside you?" he asks, his smile exuding a confidence lost on the sightless lady.

She hesitates, then apologetically whispers, "Nothing." Nodding vigorously, Oral confirms her statement. Then to the audience he exhorts, "Neighbors, put your hand on the chair in front of you as a point of contact. Let's pray together for this thing to be done—now! This moment!"

With his hands back in place, he begins praying anew. His own supplications prime the pump; soon hundreds of voices are rising and falling with his.

"Something's happening! Keep praying! Something's happening!" he encourages. After more prayer Oral releases the woman and steps back to inspect her. A photographer from a local newspaper continues to take flash pictures. The bright lights overhead are reflecting on the tears streaming from her unseeing eyes.

"Oh! I felt that," Oral says with a hearty laugh. The audience exclaims and leans forward.

"Tell us what's happening inside you."

"There—there was a light," she offered. "Sort of a flutter of light." The crowd roars approval.

As she comes off the ramp I walk over, tape recorder in hand, and identify myself as "a member of Brother Roberts' magazine staff."

"What happened to you up there on the platform?" I inquire.

"Nothing," she sobbed.

"Nothing?"

"Nothing!"

Along with the rest of the audience, I myself had been caught up in her response. I couldn't square what she was saying now with what she had said to Oral.

"Then why," *I asked amazed, "did you say what you did?"*

"I didn't want to disappoint him."

Next day the newspaper carried an eight-column spread with her picture and a headline: "'There Was a Light,' Says Blind Woman."

She didn't want to disappoint Oral Roberts . . . she wanted to *please* Oral. At the time I didn't understand. But later I did. That was an occasion when I unexpectedly found myself in Oral's grip. It happened during the recording of his worldwide radio broadcasts.

Each of Oral's radio broadcasts included a specific prayer for healing—it was the climax immediately following the sermon. Oral had this quirk: although he was praying through radio for thousands of unseen people, he wanted one visible person in front of him on whom he might focus his attention (and apply his hands!). This person, never mentioned on the air, was for Oral a representative of all those who listened. Those strong hands with their long fingers would clamp down, vise-like, on the head, shoulder, arm, or hand of the "prayee," as we assistants dubbed the vicarious model. Meanwhile, Oral would breathe concern and hope for the men, women, and children "out there in radio land."

A three-man team worked with Oral on each broadcast. While we didn't have official titles, the lines of responsibility were clear: George Woodin, production; Al Bush, promotion; and I, script. The task of finding a "prayee" was George's, and because the programs were recorded at ORU, the prayee usually was a student, professor, or staff person. When George couldn't find anyone Al and I insisted that he himself fill the spot. Although Al and I respected Oral's sincerity, neither of us wanted to be in the "prayer seat." No doubt Oral sensed our detachment, but he never commented on it or solicited our participation. Until, one day . . .

On a Saturday, five days before the next recording session, I was closing the overhead doors of my garage and the cord broke. I fell to the concrete floor, landing on my elbow. The following Monday, I went to the doctor. X-rays showed the elbow was broken.

On the taping day—Wednesday—Oral arrived late. He glanced at the cast on my arm but said nothing about it. When prayer time came and the designated student prayee stepped forward, Oral waved him aside and motioned for me instead. I glanced at Al, who was smothering a laugh. I was sure he had arranged this, and I gestured a threat his way. (Later, he assured me he was innocent.)

I had watched Oral pray for thousands of people across America and in England, Israel, Africa, Canada, and Latin America, but never before had he prayed for me. (Nobody could fault Oral on his praying; even Al and I, who treated those sessions lightly, recognized that Oral's prayers were genuine.)

It was an experience I'll never forget. In the past I had admired his forceful language, biblical imagery, and intensity, but not until I found myself in the role of prayee could I fully appreciate the magnetism and fervor, the compassion and motivation, of his outpouring.

It was a happening like no other religious experience.

When the prayer was over and we were "off the air," I found myself suffering a loss of words, and said simply, "Thanks, Oral." (Had he, after all, prayed for *me?*) He asked how I had broken the elbow and what the doctor had said. Yes, I was in his prayer, there was no doubt about it. The next day when I entered the studio for us to record again, I had an uncomfortable feeling. Somehow, I felt *guilty* wearing that cast. Oral hadn't suggested that I take the cast off (he hadn't even prayed for me, straight on), but the net effect was I felt bad because I hadn't been healed. (This despite the fact that I didn't believe in faith healing for myself.) In that moment, I understood what happened in crusades: the thousands who came desperately wanted healing and they equally needed to *please* Oral, to gain his affirmation.

A second major factor in Oral's capacity to motivate is his constant emphasis on *hope*—as distinct from optimism or positive thinking. Many people, misunderstanding Oral's emphasis on abundant living and impressed by the positiveness of his language, liken his philosophy to that of Norman Vincent Peale. Not so. As Oral understands Christian faith, there is a vast difference between hope and optimism. You won't find *optimism* (or positive thinking) in either the Old or New Testament, but *hope* appears in the Bible 125 times.

Oral never gives up *hope*. I learned this while I was minister of a Methodist church in suburban Oklahoma City. One of my first pastoral visits was to a lady who was dying in the hospital. Through the next few months, we developed mutual trust. She grew progressively worse, and several weeks before she died, she asked a favor: "Will you write Oral Roberts and ask him to pray for me? Everyone else—the doctors, my family—has given up hope. Nobody believes I'm going to get any better. But Oral Roberts, he never quits believing."

The letter was written, and five days later she received a typewritten response bearing Oral's signature (and I received one expressing appreciation for my intermediary role) and inviting me to ask assistance in the future. I recognized them to be form letters; still I was impressed by the content and the personal tone. The only source of hope for this dying lady in those last days was the letter and enclosed material sent by Oral Roberts.

It's that way for millions of other lonely, desperate people. They write to him for help, revealing their desperate need; they give to him generously; and they receive one thing especially in return: *hope*. Oral Roberts' greatest skill is to motivate people—even to find hope when there seems to be none.

CHAPTER **2**

His Sense of Personal Destiny: One Among Four Billion

ORAL ROBERTS is possessed by a sense of destiny; he has an extraordinary vision of his place in the scheme of things. One thing he believes more than anything else—as much as he believes the Bible or the creeds of the church: he has been called of God, "to bring healing to my generation." There are times when Oral will permit his methods to be questioned and new ideas to be suggested; he often has taken unfair criticism without rebuttal—but the matter of his being a "called" person is not open to discussion.

At times it's been difficult even for Evelyn, his wife, to

accept the implications of her husband's calling, and I recall an occasion when she spoke of these problems quite frankly. Oral and Evelyn, and Sharon and I were in Paris, and we were dining at one of the beautiful hotels near the Champs Elysees. That afternoon Oral and I had played a round of golf (one of the best ways for him to relax), while Evelyn and Sharon visited the Louvre. In a few days we would be flying to London for his crusade in Methodist Central Hall, Westminister. But now, in a rare moment, he was both willing and able to relax and socialize.

Evelyn's disclosure followed Sharon's relating how much she was missing our 18-month-old daughter back home. We had called home to hear her say "hello" and "bye-bye" to the tune of $50.15. That caused Evelyn to tell of her own problems raising a family of four. When Oral asked her to travel overseas with him, she was always torn between duty to her husband and her obligations to her children. Once, when she had accompanied him to Australia, Richard, the third child, protested by taking a hatchet and chopping down his bed. But it was the older son, Ronald, who suffered most. The resentment over the constant separation from his father probably contributed heavily to the gulf that still seems to separate the two of them.

"The hardest thing I had to learn," Evelyn said in summation, "was that nothing comes before Oral's ministry—not me, not the children, no one." There was no anger or recrimination in her voice; she was simply stating a fact learned during a long, hard journey.

"The only thing I refused to give in on," she said, "was that no matter where he was or what he was doing, he had to be home for the birth of our children. And he always was."

Oral smiled and clasped his hands under his chin in a

mock angelic pose. But the point was stated clearly from someone who knew best: Oral's calling—his ministry of *praying* for people—comes first.

Few people have been as identified with praying as has Oral Roberts. His sermons have been praised, his books read by millions; but those who follow him know that his praying is the keystone of his ministry. I want to distinguish between his pray*ers* and his pray*ing.* Prayers can stand alone, but praying is the act of a person. Though his pray*ers* are always thoughtful and sometimes provocative and worthy of emulation, they lack the force of his pray*ing.*

Oral's praying has awed even cynics and critics. A memorable occasion was the World Congress on Evangelism in Berlin, 1966, two years before he joined The Methodist Church. Billy Graham's personal invitation for Oral to attend brought surprise and criticism from some participants. Their reaction wasn't new or unexpected. Ultrafundamentalists had alternately picked at and bombarded Oral throughout his ministry. One criticism of most of the complainers came from their response to him on television or in the crusades. They were to discover that Oral Roberts in *person* was something else! Although his role was to have been minor, he became a center of attention. A panel that he moderated was overrun. Everywhere he went, people "rubbernecked" (a favorite phrase of Oral's). They crowded to meet him, ask his opinion, or relate an experience with healing. The warmth of his smile and contagiousness of his interest blunted the critics' arrows. But the crowning event was Oral's praying near the closing of the convention.

Dr. Graham was the main speaker, and in response to

the reception that had been accorded Oral, he asked him to offer prayer preceding the sermon.

Here were the two most famous evangelists of the twentieth century. The contrast was striking. One was a friend of presidents and foreign rulers; the other had courted the friendship of heads of state with only minor success. One was supported by the rich and powerful; the other mostly by the poor and the aged. One was best known for his preaching; the other for his praying. One used his voice; the other depended equally upon his hands. One had enjoyed generous public acceptance; the other had often suffered reproach. Graham, almost Scandinavian in appearance with his deep tan and blond hair; Oral, part Indian, with jet black hair. One a member of America's largest Protestant denomination (Southern Baptist); the other a member of one of the smallest (Pentecostal Holiness). One floated easily in the mainstream; the other found it necessary always to fight upstream.

When Oral Roberts prayed, few of those assembled had ever heard his equal. No thee's nor thou's, but in direct and forceful language he prayed as one who had been given special authority and portfolio. At the close, he hurled his words; they impacted as might giant letters splattering upon a screen:

> Satan, I come against you in the name of Jesus Christ of Nazareth, whose I am and whom I serve. I command you to take your hands off God's property NOW! In this moment! We pray and we believe. Amen.

The entire congregation was moved. Next day, the plane carrying Graham to London malfunctioned upon landing, but nobody was injured. Some who had remained for the congress to conclude, when they heard about the mishap, credited Oral Robert's prayer.

The prayer I remember most vividly he prayed in 1972 for Sharon. Oral, Evelyn, Sharon, our $3\frac{1}{2}$-year-old daughter, Laura Beth, and I had gone with Oral to Honolulu, where he was to have surgery on his sinuses.

Although Oral loves Oklahoma, it's one of the worst states for someone suffering from hay fever and allergy. Until 1965, to avoid the pollen and dust, Oral usually spent the fall in California. But with the opening of ORU, he felt it imperative to be on hand each fall. He plied himself with allergy shots and antihistamines, but he suffered just the same.

In 1970 during his trip to Japan to tape a television special, the plane refueled in Honolulu. Oral was suffering so, he disembarked, called the physicians' exchange, and located an allergist who would see him. The doctor examined him and gave him a shot for temporary relief. He recommended that Oral stop by on his return and undergo a more detailed examination. The ultimate result was surgery on the upper sinuses with the expectation of the same procedure on the lower tract within a year or two. That time came, in February, 1972.

Because I had the same symptoms, Oral requested that I accompany him along with our wives, so that I could be examined and possibly have surgery. Fortunately, the doctor did not recommend surgery for me, so Oral went into the hospital solo.

As Evelyn will tell you, Oral is one of the world's worst patients. No wonder he prays for the sick! He hates to be sick; not only that, he makes everyone around him miserable. This time it took all of us to cater to his needs and whim. I made repeated excursions for magazines, newspapers, and food—especially prunes.

Only four days after surgery, Oral convinced his physician and a relieved hospital staff that he was ready to leave. I picked him up Saturday morning. By Saturday afternoon, restless and impatient, he was pacing the floor of his hotel suite. Oral loves horses (thoroughbreds and quarter horses). He can recite with ease the bloodline of any winning horse in the past decade. Maybe that explains partially his love of Western motion pictures— especially John Wayne flicks. That night, John Wayne's "The Cowboys" was having its Honolulu premiere, and Oral insisted he was up to going. I purchased tickets.

When the four of us arrived at the theater, we confronted a long line of people waiting to be admitted who also had purchased tickets. I have never known Oral to wait in a line for anything or anybody. He simply took Sharon by the arm—she was seven and a half months pregnant—and began pushing her forward, responding to questioning glances with, "She needs to get in quick."

The movie lifted Oral's spirits, and he invited us to come to his room the next day to watch his Sunday morning television program. When the program went off, Oral abruptly said, "Let's pray." It was as if Oral hadn't been able to pray for anyone for a week; like an alcoholic in need of a drink, he needed to pray.

The four of us stood, with little Laura Beth gazing in fascination at Oral. We held hands while Oral prayed for everyone who came to mind—his "partners," as he called the millions who financially supported his ministry, his trustees, and many of his employees and regents. Then his family, and especially his only grandson, Jon Oral Nash. In the prayer, little Jon Oral was "the manchild." (When Richard and Patti's baby was born, Oral called the hospital from a motel in Los Angeles. When Patti told him he had a granddaughter and apologized for not having a boy, he responded, "That doesn't matter." But when he put down the phone, he turned to me and said, "But it does.")

Now Oral laid his hands on Evelyn. In his prayer, he declared his love for her and thanked God for all she meant to "the ministry." Problems that she faced, areas in which she needed encouragement—he dealt with a spectrum of such concerns.

Then he moved to Sharon. First, he placed his hands on the sides of her head and asked God's blessings for her, for her parents, whom he knew well, and for Laura Beth and me. Still praying, he took her hand and placed it on her stomach and prayed for our unborn child with a warmth and compassion that was incredibly moving. (His prayer was so direct, so compelling, that Laura Beth shyly peeked between the small fingers which covered her eyes, hoping to be able to see the prayed-for baby!) When he finished, Sharon's eyes were full of tears.

Finally, Oral prayed for me. Again, he expressed genuine care and concern. And of all my images of Oral, the warmest is our standing together in a motel room on that island in the Pacific, with Oral praying as nobody else can. Oral has a calling—to pray.

CHAPTER 3

"Write Me, Personally . . ."

EVERY MAN has weaknesses, and Oral has his. The one which creates most of his serious problems is his propensity to let the end justify the means. Not just *any* means, I hasten to add, because I've seen him turn down gifts of hundreds of thousands of dollars for the university because unacceptable strings were attached, and many's the time he has refused to accept large gifts from widows when their children didn't approve. He is as honest with a dollar as any man living—indeed, using popular criteria, he would earn all A's on a report card in areas of morality. But when it comes to cutting corners in procedural matters to fulfill his ministry, he has been willing to adapt and adjust to expediency.

One place where he has "bent" is the mail, which is the lifeline of the Oral Roberts organizations. The mail is at once both the biggest headache and the best cure for headaches. More than eighty-five percent of the Association's revenue comes in letters—from all over the globe. Several years ago, facing the seemingly impossible problem of handling the staggering deluge of mail, Oral adopted a rationalization that has "worked," but has also drawn criticism ranging from rebuke to ridicule.

In the late forties, Oral could personally answer the trickle of mail that came in; but once he began to cultivate his list, in a matter of months there was no way he could read and respond to the torrent that inundated him. By the mid-seventies the number of letters received in one year passed six million and has been increasing ever since. On a Monday following a television special the post office will deliver as many as 100,000 letters stuffed in dozens of sacks. Obviously, this volume requires a vast and dependable system for processing the contents.

Let me explain the sophisticated direct-mail program in use at the Oral Roberts Association in Tulsa. As you will see, it contains some very interesting (and seemingly incongruous) components relating to security and work quotas, as well as the element that provokes accusations of misrepresentation. But the system works; and executive staff members regularly participate in the Direct Mail Marketing Association's seminars and conferences to stay abreast of current trends in mailing.

First, the mail pours into the "opening room," where a machine slits the envelopes and conveys them onto an assembly-line table at which scores of women sit. As envelopes are emptied, security cameras peek over their shoulders, enabling supervisors in remote locations to police the activity. Because videotapes are made, department heads are able to spot check the operations and, additionally, to watch the watchers. (The rationale? To keep honest people honest—and to prevent misunderstandings.) The workers note the amount of the contribution (check, money order or cash) at the top of the letter, which they initial. The components are clipped together and piled in units of twenty-five, around which rubber bands are placed.

These batches are delivered to the "Letter-Analysts," one of the Association's largest divisions and the one whose employees have the most seniority—several have more than twenty years' service. Because of the intimate nature of the letters, the analysts, chosen for their maturity and commitment, feel closely related to the people who write.

This department is the heartbeat of the organization. Each analyst has a daily quota of letters, 15 to 20 units of letters, or around 425 letters per day, to read in their entirety and decide what answer "Brother Roberts" will send. Over the years, the Association has encountered just about every human problem imaginable, and appropriate answers to each category have been prepared and coded.

On a printed "topper" sheet, which lists the repertoire of coded replies, the analyst routinely writes the name and address of the letter writer, then conscientiously indicates with a checkmark the paragraphs that are to serve as a reply, and where appropriate mentions the amount of money received. (This, incorporated into the letter, will serve as a receipt for the donor.) If an additional individualized comment is required, the letter is passed on to a senior letter-analyst who writes the needed statement on the bottom of the topper sheet. The completed topper sheets are taken to a computer preparation room.

Until 1959, the toppers went to an "Auto Type" room, where two hundred typists—each tending three automatic typewriters—did the replies. Then in 1959, the Association underwrote the cost for the development of a computer chain which for the first time gave computer printers the capacity for printing letters in upper and lower case. Before that computer-produced letters were all caps.

Until recently the letter analysts' selected messages were relayed to the computer by keypunch operators; now a battery of operators sit at consoles with Cathode Ray Tubes which are hooked up to the computer miles away in downtown Tulsa. When the name of the letter writer is typed on the console, the history of that person's most recent transaction with the association is flashed upon a screen. This information enables the operator to ascertain that names and addresses are correct and makes it possible to avoid duplication of letters and paragraphs. The code indicated by the analyst is entered, and the computer is soon printing the letter at an incredible speed. After the forms are "burst," a multi-stop inserting machine quickly has the letter, enclosures and a return envelope inserted; postage is applied and a truck takes the envelope to the post office. Soon the postman has delivered the looked-for "answer from Oral."

Compare the above system with how Suzie Jones in some Northwestern city perceives it. Her husband has a severe drinking problem. One Sunday morning she watches Oral's television program. At the end he earnestly invites his viewers to write him.

"If you have a problem, I want to know about it. I will pray for God to send an answer, a miracle if necessary. For I believe in a miracle-working-God. All you need to do is write me, Oral Roberts, Tulsa, Oklahoma 74102. I'll read your letter and I'll pray for your need and write you right back."

To Suzie there's no doubt that she has a problem. She

does need help, so she sits down and starts to write a short letter requesting prayer. Before long she has spilled out her life's problems in page after page. She drops it in the mail and within a week and a half an answer is received. Her letter has an inside address, a personal salutation, and every question is treated. In words brimming with religious fervor and confidence her problem is addressed. To Suzie, "Brother Roberts" has read her letter, prayed for her, written her back and there's his signature to prove it.

Being new to the system, Suzie had not enclosed any money the first time, but she felt so good writing the letter "to someone who really understood" and wrote her back that she decides to write again, and this time she encloses a small gift (the average gift from those who respond to a Sunday morning telecast ranges between $4 and $6). Over the weeks and months, that *process* is duplicated again and again until at the end of a given year several million people have participated.

One can presume that most of these millions like Suzie hear him saying "I, Oral Roberts, will read your letter, and I, Oral Roberts, will write you." The truth is, Oral reads no more than one letter in ten thousand. The exceptions are regents, trustees, Methodist Bishops and leaders, super donors, selected Tulsans, and politicians.

And one can also presume that most of the people who receive these letters (*categorized*, if not *personalized*) say to themselves and their families and friends, "Oral Roberts took the time to read my letter, think about my problem (or, share in my joy), and write me about it—personally." Keep in mind that as a group, most of these people are women over 55 and: (1) are sold on Oral Roberts and are therefore unsuspicious, and (2) aren't as familiar with the artifices of business mail-handling as are many of their fellow citizens.

The defense or rationale for the process is that without

the assurance of personal attention, many people would never write. The results—the good things that people testify the letters bring—are sufficient validation of the *end*. Why quibble over the *means*? That's Oral's stance. Too, the system assures accessibility, an essential to one who identifies himself as specially chosen by God as His instrument of healing for this generation.

But the question is: did these millions perceive the process as Suzie did *or as* it really is? Is it subterfuge? A sham? A fraud? Critics have variously called Oral's mail system these and other names. But Oral persists. The end, in his opinion, justifies the means—the *only* means available to him. He was faced with a choice. He could: (1) stop the flow of letters—or, (2) he could receive them, take the money out and dispose of them unread—or, (3) he could adopt a method that allowed him to offer counsel and prayer (often in his own words; and, if not his own words, words that associates familiar with his thinking and style could relay in his behalf). He chose the last option—a system for coping, albeit an imperfect one.

In Oral's defense, we all bend at times. We lie to the sick and dying. Doctors sometimes do. We feign interest in problems in which we are not one whit concerned. Businesses have reply systems—#1, #2, #3, #4—to handle requests and complaints. As a writer I've received printed rejections that seemed very friendly, yet were number-coded replies signed "The Editors," or the editor's name with initials. We get computer printed letters of solicitation that are very personal sounding ("You have been selected for membership in the . . .") but have the fatal flaw of misspelling our name or improperly putting us in a category to which we don't belong.

But, perhaps, the reason the Oral Roberts system seems specious is that its fundamental tenet is geared to one man. There is never any suggestion that it's an organization or corporation dedicated to helping people, rather, it's one man doing it all. The best analogy is to Santa Claus and his helpers. Now and then you hear of Mrs. Claus and once in a while about his helpers. But to every little child awaiting the Christmas Eve visit, Santa Claus is the whole show.

The Direct Mail Marketing Association is an organization of commercial mailers, fundraisers and non-profit groups, concerned both with upgrading and policing this multi-billion dollar industry. After reflecting on some of their principles I came up with questions like these:
Does Oral intend to deceive?
Does he benefit by the deception?
Does the recipient have cause to believe something other than what's actually happening?
Is the "personal" representation of the system what moves one to respond and contribute?

The questions Oral asks, though, are:
Does it work?
Are people helped?
Are they hurt?
Are needs met that would go unmet were it not for this system?

That's the conundrum. And Oral has at times made valiant attempts to be integrally involved in the mail. Back in 1968 and 1969 there was a tremendous backlash to Oral's joining The Methodist Church. People didn't understand his reasons for this switch, and the most substantial proof was in a dramatic drop in income. Eight months after his decision, income had dropped almost a third.

Before the bottom was reached management undertook some drastic cost-cutting measures. Amenities that had been enjoyed were eliminated; support staff was reduced, and overall employment at the Association was slashed to three hundred.

Oral had always decreed, "No distinction between the millions who write and enclose no money and those who do." The no-money mail received the same careful attention. Al Bush, then Executive Vice President, had another proposal—one that would produce tremendous savings, reduce computer time, staff, supplies, postage: *Don't treat mail without money the same way as mail with money.* His recommendation was to design several printed form letters to be mailed to people who failed to enclose money. Only the correspondence with currency would go through the letter analyst system.

Oral was adamant against the shortcut. His response was very brief, very firm: "The day that becomes necessary we will stop answering any mail!"

As an alternative and with the help of Gene Ewing (another chapter), he determined to "get back into the mail." A very plain office was prepared for him. Its only furnishings were a chair, a stand for his writing supplies, and a table on which to stack letters. But there was something extraordinary about the room—the walls. From floor to ceiling they were papered with life-sized faces of people.

When I heard of his request for "people pictures," I was baffled. They were to be pictures "with feeling," and they were to be big. I assigned two editorial persons to go through the ten year file of our magazine. The photography department pulled the negatives and did blow-ups, and the graphics department soon produced a cyclorama of people—old people, young people, crippled people, healthy people, mothers in aprons, fathers working, sons on crutches, daughters playing. It was a cross-section of the world, and each photo told a story. The photos were Oral's inspiration; they enabled him to get a relevance and directness into his letters.

Oral was determined to answer personally at least one hundred letters a week, selected by the supervisors and department heads on the basis of their being "representative." Oral's one hundred answers were coded and used as responses to other correspondents. Evelyn and four trusted senior letter analysts created letters to cover topics that Oral missed.

His involvement was a key factor in a turnaround. By the end of 1969 income had doubled to over $12 million.

For Oral, a personalized, pertinent letter—answering all the questions and offering prayer for specific needs—was of the essence. A compromise would violate a public trust and his own principles. The system continues to operate, and it continues to bring hope and gratification to millions of lonely people, most of them old, many of them sick. To them the mail man is a welcome sight, and a communication from Oral Roberts is treasured! But it's not quite what they think it is. Regardless of the good it may do, it's a rationalization . . . an honest attempt to use impersonal technology to bring hope to the masses.

CHAPTER **4**

Can Oral Roberts Heal?

WHEN ORAL is challenged, "Can you heal?" he answers without equivocation, "No, I cannot heal. Only God can heal."

Then why all the palaver? If only God can heal, why not importune Him directly? Oral's standard answer to that question is, "God uses instruments." To quote him, "Without God, man cannot; without man, God will not." Or to put it more personally, "Without God, I cannot; without me, He will not." In other words, healing by faith depends on God *and* man. There is a reciprocity among the source, the instrument and the recipient. Oral quite unabashedly considers himself an instrument for the healing of the sick.

Historically, a great many Christians believe God has set apart selected individuals to perform certain ministries and missions. In both testaments, it's related that God called on prophets—first from among the Israelites, then the Christians. Lay people and clergy were ordained to perform certain vital tasks as instruments of His divine purpose. It is in this tradition that Oral assumes that God selected him as an instrument to bring healing to his generation. In his view, this selection justifies the attention that is given him and even the continuing promotion of him as a personality—it enhances his availability to the people who need him.

Can Oral Roberts, the Instrument, bring healing? Many intelligent, educated people will swear to you that they were helped by Oral; not only this, it was *only* through his instrumentality that they were healed.

In·press conferences and interviews Oral is frequently asked:

"Isn't it true that most of the people who claim they were helped by your prayers had psychosomatic illnesses?" In other words, "Wasn't their sickness all in their head?"

Oral's response is twofold: First, "I'm not a doctor, so I'm not qualified to make a medical diagnosis." Secondly, "When someone tells me they hurt and want prayer, I'm not going to tell them the pain is not real, or that it is all in their head. If they say they hurt, I believe it. And if they ask for my prayers, I'll pray for them. And whatever the cause of their illness, I'll try to believe for their healing."

Within that understanding, Oral has been successful at helping people believe for healing. He estimates that of those he prayed for, at least fifteen per cent were helped in a tangible way. Many of those I could vouch for.

One I remember especially was a young woman with epilepsy. She was twenty years old, black, and a junior in college. I remember the beauty of her doe-like eyes, whose softness seemed to contradict the violence of her distressing problem. She was under a doctor's care and taking heavy doses of prescribed drugs daily. While in the prayer line she suffered a *grand mal* (major) seizure that caused her to fall to the sawdust, writhing and babbling. When she recovered she was highly embarrassed; nevertheless, she went through the prayer line. Oral asked her name and illness. When she said epilepsy, he spent extra time with her. He explained to her and the audience that one of his sisters had been afflicted with epilepsy, and he knew the heartbreak it brought.

As he put his hands on her head, he asked the people to join him in prayer by placing their hands on the back of the chair in front of them. Then, for a few seconds, he prayed for her to "be healed and made whole." She walked off the ramp in tears. I asked her what had happened to her during his prayer. Without hesitation, she answered, "I was healed of epilepsy."

When, six months later, it was time for me to write up that crusade and check out the testimonies, she was the first person I contacted. "How's your epilepsy?" I asked. She assured me she no longer had it. Following the crusade she had gone to her physician to verify her recovery. He instructed her to continue her medication, but subsequently the drug made her sick and he gradually withdrew it. Soon, she was without medicine of any kind—yet her epilepsy did not recur.

Like Oral, I'm no doctor. I don't know a great deal about epilepsy—I do know that in some persons seizures are triggered by emotional upset. Be that as it may, I do understand that six months after Oral prayed for this young woman who had a clinically diagnosed case of epilepsy, she no longer had symptoms. Her pastor and mother both signed forms verifying the remission.

Another case got into our files quite by accident, due to

the manner in which the magazine staff covered the crusades. It was a system dictated in part by the way in which people were prayed for. Directly below the platform from which Oral preached was a ramp which ran parallel with the platform. It was engineered to a specific height so that Oral could sit in a chair on the platform and yet have eye-to-eye contact with those on the ramp as they passed by to be prayed for.

A staff photographer was positioned in front of Oral and the ramp; then at the end of the ramp an editorial person with a tape recorder waited to interview those who had been prayed for.

Routinely, most persons who came onto the prayer ramp were photographed, and the editor or reporter covering the crusade obtained the person's name for possible use in one of our publications. By virtue of past experience, Jim and Vernon, the photographers, and we writers could gauge which types were good "copy" and which weren't. However, to avoid any semblance of discrimination, the photographers often took pictures they knew we wouldn't use, and sometimes they even faked shooting someone (mainly so Oral would think they were busy). After every crusade hundreds of pictures would have been taken. It was the editorial staff person's task to be able to identify each one. It was crucial, therefore, to know the name and some identifying factor of every exposure.

On this particular night there was a teen-ager whose problem was "demon possession." As I heard him say this, I automatically dismissed him from my mind. There was no way I would put anything about demons in any article I wrote. Although I was only a summer employee working as an editorial assistant, I was determined to let this one pass by. Personally, I didn't believe in the existence of demons or in demonic possession, although we could count on several "cases" in every crusade. Moreover, Oral seemed a bit skeptical, too. He indicated to us that he seldom believed that the people who came before him were actually possessed, although he never totally contradicted them. Generally, he would make a brief statement to the audience about his beliefs on the matter: "To be demon-possessed is to declare that Jesus did his miracles by the devil. It is not emotional illness, sinfulness, or acting strangely."

He skillfully interviewed this young man who had a deep fear of the dark and of people. He didn't like people, and they didn't like him. Three times he had attempted suicide; hospitalization was the result on each occasion. He had concluded that he was demon-possessed, and he desperately wanted help. With great compassion, Oral prayed that the young man would no longer be afraid and that he would become capable of loving people and being loved in return.

Fascinating as his story was, I was planning to ignore him when Jim nodded to me, indicating that he had photographed him. Reluctantly, I conducted a brief interview, meanwhile mentally noting to tell Jim to "skip the demons from now on."

Several months later when it was time to turn in the article, the identified pictures and testimony, I checked with the managing editor. He asked for six pages on the crusade. When I checked my notes, I discovered I didn't have that much material. I went back to the photographer's contact sheets in search of additional subjects. There were a dozen good pictures of the young man, and on a long shot, I gave him a call.

I asked permission to interview him for *Abundant Life Magazine,* and he said, "Certainly." There was an easy confidence in his voice.

"How are you now?"

"I'm great, and I wish everyone were like me!"

I didn't have to ask any more questions. He spilled out a story of no longer being afraid of the dark, of loving people and having friends. There was only one restriction: he did not want the article to say he was healed of demon possession. He realized now he had misunderstood his problem. As he and others vouchsafed, he was a totally changed person from the fearful man of months ago.

The third healing was the recovery of an alcoholic. This man awakened from a two-week binge to find himself two thousand miles from home. Broke, without a job, knowing nobody, he made his way to the Oral Roberts crusade seeking prayer. The story that unfolded was a familiar one: divorce (with a second one pending), inability to keep a job, no sense of direction. Futility.

Months later, when I phoned his home, his wife blurted out that her husband was a changed man. He had a good job and had been on the wagon ever since the crusade. She had dropped the divorce proceedings.

These three cases have psychosomatic implications. But what about persons diagnosed as having terminal illness who claim to have been healed through prayer and faith? Is that kind of healing obtainable through "instruments," including Oral Roberts?

In studying scores of cases and interviewing hundreds of people, I have seen the following pattern emerge: Upon being told they had a terminal illness, many patients didn't believe it and went to other doctors hoping for a brighter diagnosis. Either this, or they decided to ignore the diagnosis, hoping the problem would go away.

Finally, when no alternative presented itself, they submitted to the therapy prescribed by their physician. In cancer, this usually involved surgery, radiation, and/or chemotherapy. Often, because of the impact of the treatment, their bodies reacted in such a way that they seemed to be worse instead of better. Impotent, weak, nauseous, they suspected their doctor had failed them. In desperation, they turned to Oral Roberts.

I've seen them in the "Invalid Room" tent, lying on a stretcher or cradled in the arms of a mother or father, hoping against hope that a five or ten-second touch by Oral Roberts would somehow bring health once again. A few claimed to have found it. They were dying—Oral Roberts prayed for them—and now they were alive and well!

On those rare occasions when I could persuade the doctors to comment on these cures, they stressed the prior therapy the patient received. Oral's prayers? Often, the comments were unprintable.

Yet, some patients actually experienced a discernible change for the better, and the recovery couldn't always be handily assigned to the treatment. Any doctor worth his salt will tell you that mental attitude is an essential component in combating a major illness. Some patients virtually will themselves to die—and they do. Others exhibit courage and determination and thereby survive the direst of prognoses.

One of the best examples of determined survival relates to a person who credited her turnabout to Oral's close friend, the late Kathryn Kuhlman. Kathryn achieved national prominence before her death, and Oral saw her as having been divinely selected to fill the void left when he discontinued his crusades. (At the time this was being written, she was in a Tulsa hospital for heart surgery, and Oral was reported to be at her side during the long operation. She died before proof pages were sent from the printer.) Kathryn was a remarkable woman, probably in her seventies, though her age was a well-guarded secret.

In 1972, I was asked to consider writing a book for her. I confided to the person representing her that I had met her only briefly and had heard her speak only once, and I wasn't overly impressed on either occasion. I had a very limited picture, he said. Kathryn was "quite different." Doctors sat on the platform and verified her healings, he related.

I agreed to do the book provided that I was satisfied with data relating to what was acclaimed as the greatest healing of her entire ministry. As a preliminary project, I would produce a magazine article on the case which the intermediary assured me had been documented by physicians and hospitals as being truly miraculous.

The subject told a moving story. Consumed by cancer, she had been on the brink of death. Then she experienced a remission. But before the remission she had treatment, later followed by Kathryn's prayers. To what should her remission be attributed? Was it the doctors' treatment—or Kathryn Kuhlman's prayers? The patient testified that she had suffered even more extremely while undergoing a series of radical treatments, and out of desperation she turned to Kathryn Kuhlman. While attending one of her crusades she felt a miraculous change for the better. After that, her strength returned and her whole attitude towards life brightened. The six months she had been given to live had passed, yet here she was, alive and healthy. Indeed, she was kept busy testifying at Kathryn Kuhlman's crusades.

When I checked with the doctors, I found none of the

open enthusiasm I'd been promised. After some rebuffs, I managed to speak with two doctors—one who had been the primary physician, the other a member of the hospital staff. Had their patient been healed by Kathryn Kuhlman—or them?

Their explanation was that radical treatment nearly always produces debilitating side-effects while the body adjusts. They had no doubt about it: their patient's remission resulted from the application of medical science. And the efforts of the faith healer? Irrelevant and immaterial, they asserted. They said they knew what their patient was like before treatment and what the treatment could be expected to do. They also knew where she would be without that treatment! They deplored her faith-healing testimony, fearing that it might mislead others and cause them to delay treatment.

I wrote the story and emphasized the patient's change in attitude as a result of Kathryn's prayers. When I sent it to Kathryn for review, she protested that I had totally missed the point! Naturally, I never wrote the book.

Can Oral Roberts, Kathryn Kuhlman, or any such person invoke healing? If Oral were analyzing the above story, he probably would credit the roles of both Kathryn and the medical team. Several times I have heard him tell of his own healing from tuberculosis. He was under the care of three physicians, and in retrospect he credits both the treatment of the physicians and the prayers of a traveling evangelist. Oral refuses to pit faith healing against medical science; indeed, he himself remains under a physician's care. With him the key to health isn't either/or, but both/and.

I doubt if Oral believes some of the way-out transformations claimed by colleagues. I recall his reaction to the first story I ever consulted him about. It was dramatic! A young man had come into the invalid room with an angry infection on his leg. As Oral prayed for him, the sore began to dry up—right before our reporter's very eyes.

The established procedure on the magazine was to validate cases through interviews with the subject and others—family, neighbors, physicians, or pastor. The system slipped and green on the job as the new editor, I queried the reporter closely, but sent the article to be typewritten without external screening.

When I showed Oral the page proofs, he read the episode and demanded, "Wayne, did you check that out?"

I answered that I had checked with the reporter, and she had sworn to me that it happened as she related it.

"I was there and I didn't see it," he retorted. "In twenty years of praying for people, I've never seen anything like that happen."

After that, I felt more comfortable, more secure, about covering Oral's crusades. He had given me notice that he didn't want any exaggerated claims of healing, and I was glad.

CHAPTER 5

Millions of Dollars—For Whom?

WHEN ORAL'S detractors have finished assailing his claim to be a healing agent and his fondness for publicity, they turn to that root of all evil . . . money. Some of Oral's critics might dismiss questioned principles and practices as being mere academic issues were it not for his huge financial success. People ask: Is Oral Roberts wealthy? A multi-millionaire? Does he profit from people's misfortunes?

At the outset, let me state that Oral has never once charged anyone for his prayers; neither has there ever been any financial stipulation before he would pray for a person. That would be repugnant to him. Occasionally, I hear stories to the contrary, and I spike them by offering double the amount of money allegedly given Oral if the tale can be proved. I've yet to lose a cent.

But the issue of his financial success is relevant. Somehow it just doesn't seem right for one person to live in ease and luxury simply by profiting from someone else's misfortune and misery. That holds true for anyone in any field. For example, in Oklahoma, there have been reports of physicians refusing to treat welfare patients—this despite the fact that Oklahoma taxpayers have coughed up half a million tax dollars to provide the facilities and staff necessary to train each doctor. For those doctors who have benefited from public education, rebuffing the poor seems grossly irreconcilable, especially when one looks at the expensive cars and big homes that many of those same doctors enjoy. And to make hundreds of thousands of dollars off the aged through Medicare or Medicaid is nothing to brag about either.

The same feelings prevail in regard to Oral. It just seems wrong to get rich off misfortune. But is Oral rich? There's a lot of money, but where does it go? And if Oral doesn't *charge* money for his prayers, some assert, he certainly does *persuade* people to give it to him.

The answer is threefold: First, Oral's operating premise is that if his ministry meets the needs of people, then the ministry's needs will be taken care of also. The vast apparatus of the Association is geared to that end. The mail, magazines, television, radio, and books are all designed to solve or resolve the problems for which people ask help. It's a service-oriented approach.

Secondly, Oral gives to people before they give to him. He risks receiving no return at all when he sends people books, mementos, and recordings free of charge (though reams of statistics on past giveaways insure that the return will be many times more than the cost). Every radio broadcast or television program concludes with Oral's offer to give the listener something free. Just write and ask for it. Not only is there never a charge; there's no mention made of the cost to the Association. Skeptics have discovered that every offer is, indeed, free.

Third, and this is vital: he never asks directly for gifts for himself or his ministry. Rather, he puts it this way: If *you* need help give to him. He never asks you to help him by giving to him, but help yourself by giving to him.

The thesis of the Roberts system for cultivating potential donors is based on three assumptions concerning your first communication to the Association. First, you have watched or heard Oral or you've read about him—thus, you have an interest in him. Second, you took the time to write. Third, you wanted a symbol of his ministry, whether a book, recording, or memento. The crucial aspect of developing this budding relationship is for Oral to fulfill his promise, and do so promptly. (On Oral's first prime-time television special he offered a stereo-LP free. Many doubted both the gratuitous nature of the offer and the quality of the record, and when both criteria were fulfilled, these incredulous ones were converted into candidates for future giving.) The mail department has orders not to let any letter go unanswered longer than five days. A free premium is to be sent immediately, postage paid.

The names of persons initiating an original inquiry are stored in the computer information bank (to preclude duplication of "first time" response). There's still another gift, a free three-month subscription to *Abundant Life*. This magazine contains sermons and testimonies of persons who have been helped by Oral Roberts' ministry, and promotional ads giving away still more premiums.

Three months after the first inquiry, a "personal" computer letter invites the recipient to write for prayer at any time. The emphasis is upon service and the meeting of needs. A form is enclosed on which to write a prayer request. Now we encounter the first mention of money. At the bottom of the prayer request form appears a line to the effect, "Brother Roberts, I am enclosing $— as my seed faith offering for the meeting of my needs." Although the exact wording will change from time to time, the important point for the success of the appeal is that it doesn't solicit help for anyone other than the giver—not even the Roberts ministry, though that's to whom the money goes; rather, it's phrased to recognize that the person giving is the one being helped. It's a selfish gift, in one sense, and that is one of the strongest appeals that can be made, for most of us are basically selfish. Almost invariably, we will act to take care of our own needs before we will be willing or able to take care of someone else's needs. In fact, there is psychological evidence that self-awareness and self-love are crucial prior components to helping others. Oral's request for money recognizes that reality of human nature.

The approach described has been extraordinarily successful. Despite periodic purging of the computer files to remove the names of people who haven't been heard from in the past year, at any one time those files contain millions of names, and the list continues to grow.

What part of the millions of dollars in receipts does Oral personally receive?

In the beginning there was no income from the mail; all monies received came via the crusades. In 1947 and 1948 these crusades were sponsored by individual churches, and the amount of money he received varied, depending upon the prior arrangement made with the local church. When his meetings grew so popular that one church wasn't capable of handling the crowds, Oral bought a tent and got several churches to band as sponsors of each of his meetings. To be able to accept contributions he formed a board of trustees and incorporated as "Healing Waters Ministries, Inc." Except for local expenses and followup, all money went to his organization and he decided how it was to be distributed. During this period, top members of his team shared in a percentage of the offerings.

In the mid-fifties Oral's national and international successes gave him increased visibility, and his programs on national television initiated another restructuring of his personal income system. Now, Oral received only the last offering in the crusade. It was called a "love offering for Brother Roberts," a holdover from Oral's Pentecostal Holiness Church days when a special offering occasionally would be received for the pastor above and beyond his salary. During this time, and especially in the late 1950's, Oral's income was enormous.

I once asked Al Bush, President of the Association until 1972, how much he thought Oral made in the heyday of his crusade ministry. He estimated that there probably were three years in which Oral received a million dollars a year before taxes. After that it dropped off considerably.

Oral remained on this schedule of one offering per crusade until 1962, but meanwhile his income from the sale of his books was burgeoning. These were hawked at every service by ushers who went up and down the aisles like vendors at a football game. In 1962, largely through the influence of Dr. R. O. Corvin, at one time Chancellor of ORU and later Dean of the Graduate School of Theology, Oral went on a salary of $15,000 a year. And in a move that he felt validated his financial integrity he divested himself of all his personal holdings, including his home, and put them in the endowment fund of the university. Revenue from his books now went into a trust fund for the children. For the first time since 1947 he was on a salary. Around 1967, it was raised to $19,000. Oral remarked shortly after the raise that he liked the $15,000 better, but Evelyn insisted they needed more—she kept their personal checking account and paid all the bills.

Another change occurred in 1968 following a protracted verbal duel with a Canadian newsman on television. It came during the last crusade he would hold in Canada. The people of Edmonton, British Columbia, had been receptive, and a real surprise was the warmth and acceptance of the press. In spite of his prevailing reluctance to be interviewed by newsmen, Oral accepted an invitation to appear on a regional telecast, "Face the Newsmen," which was patterned after "Face the Nation."

On our way to the station I suggested possible questions and answers. By the time we arrived he seemed confident although still reluctant and wary. The participants were three newsmen, the moderator and Oral. The first questions were predictable. Then a panelist asked Oral the amount of his salary.

"Not nearly as much as you think."

"How much."

"I gave you an answer."

Oral's reluctance made the reporter feel he had bitten into a real issue, and he pressed harder. "$100,000?"

"Oh, my Lord! No."

"$50,000?"

"You're way off."

"$25,000?"

"Of course not."

"$20,000?"

"No, but you're getting closer." (The figure was, as I've stated, $19,000.)

Exasperated, the newsman demanded quite loudly, "Well, how much is it?"

Oral was in charge now, and he still didn't want to answer. He turned the tables and asked the reporter, "How much do you make?"

The newsman blushed and mumbled his answer.

Oral said, "I can't hear you."

"$6,000."

Nodding his head, Oral said, "I see."

It was evident that newsman wished he had left the whole matter alone, and Oral was similarly embarrassed at having forced the revelation of the newsman's relatively small salary. Belligerently, the reporter inquired, "All right, I've told mine. How much do you make?"

Oral smiled apologetically and said, "Like I told you, you're close." Then he turned to the moderator as if to say, "Next subject, please."

On the plane home, Oral was still bothered by the question and he solicited my advice. We agreed that no matter how little or how much he made, a lot of people wouldn't be satisfied. And in terms of performance and value to the organization, any management consultant would concur that he was grossly underpaid. But that was more of a problem than it was a solution.

The truth of the problem was that any amount of money received under the umbrella of his healing ministry would leave him open to criticism. Yet Oral was not only maintaining a regular crusade schedule, he was also devoting a great deal of time and energy to his post of president at ORU. The solution seemed simple.

It was decided that he should no longer be paid by the Oral Roberts Evangelistic Association, but rather by Oral Roberts University, which he served as president. In that way he could honestly answer that for all his evangelistic work, the crusades, and radio and television appearances, he received no salary. As president of the university he would receive his current salary of $19,000. Somehow, Oral seemed much more comfortable with that arrangement. For the first time ever he was at ease talking about his personal finances. The proof came years later when NBC newsman Tom Petit taped an interview on campus. With no hesitation, Oral told him his salary. The exchange was edited out in the final interview as being unimportant.

In 1970, Oral's salary was raised to $24,500, slightly under the $25,000 received by Billy Graham (as Oral was prone to mention). Recently, after another increase, sources close to Oral placed it in the neighborhood of $30-$35,000. Additionally, the university provides him with a $150,000 home; the television budget provides his wardrobe; and he enjoys memberships in the elite Southern Hills Golf and Country Club and the Meadowbrook Golf and Country Club, both paid by the university. Back when he was spending considerable time on the West Coast, he also had membership in the Newport Beach Golf and Country Club, south of Los Angeles.

Generally speaking, people react to the amount of Oral's income in the way it compares to their own. People with low incomes think it far too much, while people with money regard it as extremely low. When Oral was nominated for membership on the board of directors of the National Bank of Tulsa, the president, Dr. Eugene Swearingen, expressed surprise at Oral's modest financial statement. Dr. Swearingen, who came to NBT after serving as president of Tulsa University, received a salary of $60,000 at NBT, plus very generous amenities. Many secular corporations with comparable income and assets pay their chief executives many times what Oral receives.

Several factors outside Oral's control have affected his

salary. First, while the university was struggling to gain accreditation, financial stability was a crucial criterion. The accrediting association used faculty and administrative salaries as one measure of the strength and stability of the institution. (These salaries were compared with those paid at neighboring schools.) Though Oral's salary remained less than that of other university presidents, it had to stay in the ball park. And though they do what he wants most of the time, the ORU board of regents sets Oral's salary.

Another factor is Oral's need to attract and keep capable administrative personnel at ORU and the Association. There salaries tend to be high compared to other religious organizations, but low compared to secular businesses. Oral, in the top position, has to let his salary set the scale for those below him. If his own pay is too low it depresses the salary of subordinates. Oral finally lost Al Bush, after 15 years of service, and the most capable executive he ever had, largely because Al could make much more elsewhere.

Oral's attitude toward pocket money is interesting. When you travel with him you'd better have enough money for the both of you, because he never pays for anything—meals, hotels, taxis, or Juicy Fruit gum (which he chews a pack at a time, throwing it away once the flavor is gone). And his tastes are not all that rich either. Red beans and cornbread, with green onions and tomatoes on the side, are an excellent meal for him. I remember, for instance, one evening in Portland when he came into the dining room and sat at my table where I was just beginning to bite into an expensive steak. He ordered soup!

Once Oral told me that he had never been able to make

any significant amount of money in secular enterprises. Land, cattle, farming, stocks—whatever—his investments never turned out well. In contrast, nearly every program he has attempted for the ministry has shown the Midas touch. He seems to have a hip-pocket intuition—he credits God's direction—that guides him as to when to buy and when to sell . . . but it works only for the ministry.

Oral is an extremely generous man. He gives a full ten percent of his income to Boston Avenue United Methodist Church, and he gives away his considerable speaking fees and honorariums. When his autobiography, *The Call,* was published by Doubleday, $25,000 of the $40,000 advance went to him personally. He promptly gave it to the University. Later, when the paperback rights sold for $80,000, again he gave away his share. Several years ago, his attorney told me that Oral regularly made more donations than the I.R.S. ceiling for tax deductions.

His philosophy is that the more one gives, the more he will receive, and that fundamental principle has guided where the money goes.

CHAPTER **6**

An Overseas Disaster

NOT FAR from ORU is the headquarters of another highly successful evangelist, T.L. Osborn. There's a distinct difference in the locales of their success: T. L. wows them overseas but has trouble getting a crowd in America. He isn't well known even in Tulsa, although he has a large ultramodern headquarters on U.S. Highway 66. But abroad, he's a master at gaining widespread attention of officials and enthusiastic responses from the people.

Oral hates to go overseas, is one of the world's most inept travelers, has few tourist interests (he isn't impressed by historical sites), dislikes fancy foods, and is constantly frustrated by communications difficulties. (On his first visit to Rome he was through sightseeing in less than three hours so we went to a theatre and saw Sammy Davis, Jr. and Peter Lawford in "Salt and Pepper." Though I'm no great sightseer myself, it did seem that the "Eternal City" was worth more than three hours.)

Nevertheless, despite his dislike of international travel, for many years an annual overseas crusade was considered a must. To judge by the reports in *Abundant Life* they were highly successful, but those who went along know there was another side, sometimes humorous, sometimes testing. In Nairobi, Kenya as Oral began preaching to a crowd estimated at more than 80,000, he lost his voice and Bob DeWeese had to fill in. In Australia, mobs chased him out of the country with stink bombs and threats of even more violent actions.

Oral's frustration with the time required for translation showed dramatically during his crusade in South Africa in the late 1950's. Among the 100,000 black men and women who had been herded together under the broiling sun, at least three tribal languages were represented. The translation process was necessarily cumbersome. Following every phrase, Oral had to wait for three interpretations. He couldn't get a rhythm going. Periodically, he impatiently jumped ahead of the last translator and in the ensuing confusion lost his train of thought. In desperation, he motioned to the translators to be seated. To the astonishment of the sponsoring committee and his staff, he began speaking directly to the crowd in uninterrupted English. After preaching for almost an hour, he motioned his interpreters back up and gave an altar call, with translations. Many hundreds responded. Oral felt vindicated. Later, he proudly declared that the Holy Spirit had been his interpreter.

His Chilean crusade was a memorable fiasco. During the International Congress on Evangelism in Berlin, a delegation from Chile had petitioned him, "Come to Chile and help us." Oral, flushed with the warm response of the Congress, accepted. His associate, Dr. R. O. Corvin, still Chancellor at ORU, was given responsibility for preliminary planning.

The date agreed upon was December, 1967. Satellite crusades were to be conducted throughout the nation, culminating in one gigantic rally in the nation's capital, with assurances that fifty to one hundred thousand would attend.

Over $50,000 in Association money was sent down for use in pre-crusade publicity. Reports came back that the nation was receptive—even the president was interested. This crusade, according to the contact man in Chile, would be the greatest in Oral's entire ministry. Banners, billboards, and posters were being displayed throughout Santiago, he reported, and everyone was awaiting God's man of the hour, Oral Roberts.

Our plane arrived at the Santiago airport. On it with Oral were a World Action team from Oral Roberts University, University Chaplain Tommy Tyson, Associate Evangelist Bob DeWeese, a camera crew, and I. Instead of the cheering masses that we expected, we were greeted by about fifty people holding aloft a single banner. Several Spanish-speaking ministers came up to shake Roberts' hands. The "crowd" sang some songs, our cameras rolled, and Roberts smiled—but I, for one, knew his smile was screening a seething interior.

Obviously, something was wrong, and in the car on the way to our hotel, the truth began to come out. Over the next several days, the full scandal emerged: Our advance man, an American who also was a CIA operative, had fled the country. We were now deluged by creditors. And as a coup d'etat, he had written a hot check for $1,500 to the advertising agency handling the account.

To make matters worse, with Oral's full knowledge, Dr. Corvin had, during his preliminary visits, discussed the possibility of establishing in Chile a sister university of Oral Roberts University. A fifty million dollar figure had been tossed around. This, we learned, was one of the reasons President Frei had expressed great interest in the crusade. Indeed, when we reached the hotel, reporters and cameramen were waiting to ask, "When will the university be started?"

"There will be no university," Oral responded abruptly. "The promises made by those before me were unauthorized, and I categorically reject them." (Dr. Corvin later swore to me the opposite and his evidence was most convincing.)

An invitation for Oral to visit the President the next day was withdrawn. The front pages of the local newspapers were scathing. The headlines were all variations of "roast Roberts."

Oral faithfully fulfilled the promised itinerary for satellite crusades although in cities where 5,000 were promised, only 500 showed. In some places, only handfuls gathered in barren fields.

Early in the evening before the main crusade was to begin in Santiago, there was a question whether it would open. The grounds and facilities were inadequate. There were poorly constructed stands, a monstrous cross, and four strings of light bulbs. We had been promised that tens of thousands would trek inland from the coast, push across the mountains, and come up from the south. Instead, a few thousand officially estimated at between "three to ten thousand" (which was correct if you give or take three to ten thousand) assembled and the service began. Rivalries among the many Pentecostal splinter groups resulted in less than enthusiastic participation by their leaders. Thus, the planned "choir of thousands" was a choir of hundreds.

After the preliminaries, the master of ceremonies introduced "God's man of the hour for Chile, Reverend Oral Roberts." There was much applause. Oral expressed his thanks to the people for coming. Then, as he started reading his text, the power went off and we were in total darkness. For five minutes we waited; meanwhile, Spanish-speaking ministers admonished the crowd to be patient and remain orderly. When the lights did come on again, the man at center stage wasn't Oral Roberts, but Tommy Tyson!

While Tommy preached, I circled behind the platform and found Bob DeWeese. In twenty years with Oral he thought the had seen everything—but this! Laughing, he said that Oral, complaining of diarrhea, had gone back to the hotel. This was no surpise, really, because it was always presumed that Oral's intestinal tract would suffer upset whenever he went overseas. Before leaving statewide he would take pills to prevent infection, then take others to counteract the unpleasant effects of the first ones. His system wouldn't stand that sort of tinkering.

When we got back to the hotel after the service, we learned that not only had Oral been there, but departed —at that very moment he was high in the sky on his way back to the United States of America. And, we faced five more days of the crusade!

Each night, without any explanation of Oral's absence, Tommy and Bob preached. The local ministers kept wanting to know where "Reverendo Roberts" was. Each time, the answer was, "Brother Roberts won't be here tonight." Left unsaid was the gloomy truth that he wouldn't be there *any* night.

Finally, Sunday afternoon came. A giant rally was scheduled in the capitol plaza in downtown Santiago. A parade would wind its way to the crusade grounds for the final service. Before the rally, Tommy Tyson and I went to lunch. As we ate, we commiserated over the past week's incredible miasma of hokum. We kept on talking. The time for the rally passed, then the parade, as well. Finally, we left the cafe and rode to the crusade grounds where it was Tommy's unhappy assignment following the service to explain to the ministers that their man of the hour had taken ill and had flown back to America, but that for the sake of the crusade, no public announcement had been made.

With characteristic equanimity, Tommy had the ministers join hands together and pray for Brother Roberts who was safe and sound in North America and poised to make a move that would profoundly affect his ministry. He was about to leave the Pentecostal Holiness Church.

CHAPTER 7

The First Time Oral Joined The Methodist Church

IN APRIL, 1967, two months before graduating from seminary, I was being considered for a job in New York with *Christianity & Crisis,* an exciting biweekly magazine founded by theologian Reinhold Neibuhr. My major professor in seminary, Dr. Schubert Ogden, had recommended me for the post of assistant editor. One morning the editor called to tell me he would be down on Friday of the next week to interview me. That same afternoon, Al Bush, then Executive Vice President of the Oral Roberts Association, called. Bill Armstrong, the managing editor of *Abundant Life Magazine* had resigned. I was being offered the position of Editor-in-Chief of Publications.

Incidentally, Oral had previously vowed never to have

an editor-in-chief again and for six years the top position had been managing editor, with Oral carrying the title of the editor-in-chief. There was a bitter taste in Oral's mouth from a dispute with the last editor-in-chief, who was released after being accused of alleged improprieties (more smoke than fire). The editor retaliated by preparing an "expose" of Oral for release to the wire services. There was little new information in it, but because of the way it was written it could be interpreted as detrimental to Oral. Oral went to see his Unitarian friend Jenkin Lloyd Jones, editor of the *Tulsa Tribune.* He asked "Jenk" to intercede with AP, which he did. When the AP backed off, UPI declined also, and Oral was saved considerable embarrassment.

Now Oral was ready to try again. As editor-in-chief I would have editorial responsibility for *Abundant Life Magazine,* a monthly magazine with a circulation of half a million, *Daily Blessing,* a quarterly with a circulation of over 250,000 and ORU's *Outreach* with a circulation slightly over 100,000 plus the production of books, brochures and other printed pieces numbering millions of copies monthly. Also, Oral was going to Vietnam in July and wanted me to accompany him as photographer and press liaison.

I flew to Tulsa to discuss the position with Oral. As I was to see demonstrated time and again, in one-on-one situations, Oral is a past master at persuasion—especially when you're wanting to be persuaded! Like Oral, I had the hangover of poverty from my childhood. ORU's gleaming gold and white buildings contrasted sharply with having lived with a family of seven in two rooms with a path, at the back of a church, which rooms on Sunday were again used for Sunday School; or hiding from my teenage friends the fact that I lived in three Sunday school rooms in the basement of a Pentecostal Holiness church.

But here was luxury with no expense spared. *Never mind where the money came from,* I reasoned, *there was good rationalization for that.*

When Al ushered me into Oral's sixth story office in the executive penthouse atop ORU's Learning Resources Center, I was dutifully impressed. I had been there a couple of times before during the previous two summers while employed as a temporary editorial assistant. But this was different. I could be a permanent part of all of it. The velvet chairs, the unobstructed view of Tulsa and the campus, the size and furnishings were immense. (Strangely enough, Dr. Messick, formerly Executive Vice President of ORU, had managed to have his office designed so as to be larger than Oral's. When Carl Hamilton succeeded Dr. Messick, one of the prerequisites Oral insisted on before Carl actually took office was to remodel it so as to make it smaller than Oral's!)

But the real persuader was not the office or the furnishings. It was Oral. I'm convinced that most people would fail to predict how Oral acts in a "selling" situation. His image suggests the strong, knock-down-all-resistance image. He's just the opposite.

It starts with his handshake—"the limp fish" style. There's no hard squeeze or hearty "How are you's." Rather, a quiet underplaying of strength and confidence (something like Mark Twain's definition of confidence as a "Christian with four *aces!*") A warm smile and opening words . . . within moments you have forgotten that this is world-famous Oral Roberts; rather, it's close-friend Oral, I-have-a-dream Oral, a dream-with-you-in-it Oral. Suddenly, you've convinced yourself that he honestly needs your help and, in fact, you're the only person who can really do what he needs done. And, as an extra incentive you've been offered a salary that's triple what you've ever made, an administrative assistant, an executive secretary and a clerk-typist to help you run your office.

Though an hour later I couldn't remember any of his exact words, I understood that as editor-in-chief I would have unrestricted authority and complete responsibility for running a top-flight editorial department. Needed staff would be hired. And the clincher: one of the reasons he wanted me particularly was his intention to change his image. He wanted somone with a fresh perspective to design and direct his communications program.

I accepted without having that interview with *Christianity & Crisis* (an omission I occasionally rued in the years to come). On June 1, 1967, I went to work for Oral.

As I reflect on the relationship that extended until September, 1972, several changes occurred which broke the mold of the .faith-healer image. In 1967, a decision already in the making, the old television programs were dropped with their filming of the crusades, the prayer lines and the testimonies. A year and a half later, the giant tent was folded up and put away forever. The phrases so popular in years past . . . "the world's largest tent" . . . "canvas cathedral" . . . reflected a bygone era. In 1968 he joined The Methodist Church. In 1969 his new television series began without the crusade films or televised prayers and healing. In 1970, with the hiring of Ken Trickey as coach, ORU's basketball team attracted national interest. In 1971 ORU was accredited. In 1972 his best selling autobiography was published by the publishing giant Doubleday. During that year he had the most extensive and favorable media coverage since he began in 1947.

With the exception of basketball and accreditation, I was intricately involved in those changes. And even the exceptions opened doors in phenomenal ways. Of all the changes, though, none signified a more fundamental one than his joining The Methodist Church, which may be why it created such a deep backlash. To understand the reaction requires a knowledge not only of the great disparity between his former church and The Methodist Church, but also of the events in those formative years that shaped the early Oral.

Oral was reared in the church of his parents, the Pentecostal Holiness Church. This small, extremely conservative sect was headquartered in a little town of less than five hundred population, Franklin Springs, Georgia. Although it was one of the older Pentecostal bodies, it had never experienced the phenomenal growth of other doctrinally similar groups. It had a conservative leadership, an extremely narrow social code, an unusually strong doctrine of personal holiness, and a restrictive membership policy.

Oral's father was a pioneer Pentecostal preacher. Measured over against his contemporaries, Ellis Roberts was at best a moderate success. His revivals failed to catch fire, and more than once he ended up with no money to send back home to feed his family. As Oral expressed it, "Even the poor people called us poor." But while her husband seemed non-industrious at times, Momma Roberts was a ball of fire. She prodded and pushed her husband constantly to earn enough to support their brood of six children.

Oral developed a keen awareness of the importance of money. He and his father played a game in which they watched the people as they came forward to put their money in the offering plate each Sunday morning. Once father and son were home, but before the offering was counted, they would see who could come closest to estimating the total amount given. Oral seldom lost.

When Oral was twelve they lived in Pontotoc County, Oklahoma. The local Methodist church was having a revival. Although the Robert's church frowned on child membership, the Methodist evangelist was actively soliciting the attendance and conversion of children by giving away free candy. For a poor preacher's son candy was a rare commodity, and Oral was always on hand. When the invitation to membership was made, Oral, to make sure he received the candy, went forward with his friends and joined The Methodist Church. His parents were incredulous, but the fact is that Oral first belonged to the Methodist Episcopal Church (South), one of the original bodies of the present United Methodist Church.

By the time he was sixteen, a serious rift had developed between Oral and his family. Although Oral was whipped infrequently, the corporal punishment meted out by his dad on those few occasions was severe. In Oral's words, "Papa seldom got mad, but when he did he wanted to kill you." Oral's aggressiveness and brilliance conflicted with the resignation of the world in which he lived. He dreamed of becoming a lawyer and winning the governor's office; obviously, a Pentecostal Holiness preacher's home in Pontotoc County seemed a poor place to start. Additionally, the taboos forced upon him seemed patently irrelevant to life in that make-believe world on the other side of the tracks.

A tall, skinny teenager stood defiantly at the door. "I'm leaving, Papa and Mama, and I'm not coming back. You can say what you want, but I'm not staying."

Ellis Roberts threatened, "Oral, I'll get the police to bring you back." But his sixteen year old boy was in body a man. "I'll run away again."

Before he walked out the door, Claudia Roberts

reached up to her six foot one-and-a-half inch tall son and pulled his head down on her shoulders. Sobbing, she cried, "God will send you home."

In Antlers, away from home he began to apply himself. There was a job before school, another after school and a third on weekends. Though a newcomer, he was elected junior class president. He also made the starting basketball team. Soon would come college—law school—the governor's chair—and the world. . . . But then it happened. In the Oklahoma Seven Basketball Tournament, racing down the basketball court, Oral Roberts dribbled hard trying to go in for a layup. The pain in his chest throbbed, his lungs ached as though on fire. Suddenly, he stumbled, falling hard to the floor, unconscious, his lungs hemorrhaging, and blood pouring from his mouth.

A few hours later, finding himself on the back seat of his coach's car headed back to his parents' home, Oral reached the lowest point in his life. All his dreams had collapsed.

In the wee hours of the morning the Reverend Ellis Roberts, pastor of the Stratford, Oklahoma, Pentecostal Holiness Church, heard a knock at the door. It was a man who identified himself as the basketball coach at the Antlers, Oklahoma high school. "I have your son in the car."

When Claudia Roberts saw her son's limp, blood-flecked body being carried in, she screamed, "Oh God! not that way!"

For days Oral fought for his life. At times his lungs hemorrhaged so heavily that pillows and sheets were soaked. The doctors' diagnosis was, as feared, tuberculosis. The only available remedy was a sanitarium in Eastern Oklahoma, the one in which an uncle had died.

The decision was postponed. A quarantine was imposed for a time. When his condition grew steadily worse relatives and friends whispered about the possibility of death. Ellis Roberts made his decision.

It was Wednesday night, and there would be a prayer meeting in the church next door. But, he informed Oral, the deacons would have to conduct the service. "Oral," he said, "I'm going to get down on my knees at the foot of this bed. And I'm going to start praying. God being my helper, I won't stop until you give your heart and life to Christ."

Until that time Oral had refused every religious entreaty. For a young man with stars in his eyes about the real world, there was little attraction to be found in stars in your crown in a heavenly world to come. Years later, when writing and preaching about healing, he would demonstrate an appreciation for sick people's concern to live in this world, not another world. Life now, not an eternal tomorrow!

Oral relates that he lay unmoved, even resentful of his father—and God. He hated his sickness and sickbed. He wanted to get up, be well, live his own life. He glanced at the foot of the bed. His father's eyes were closed, tears spilling down his cheeks, his voice uplifted in prayer. As he watched, his father's face was transformed into the face of Christ.

Suddenly, the years of conditioning—hymns, prayers and sermons—took their effect. The rebellious young man, who had rejected his parents, the church, and God, suddenly wanted to be accepted by them all. Oral leapt to his feet. Standing on his bed, arms upraised, he cried out for Jesus to save him. The first step in his transformation was complete.

But he was still sick. His parents may have been satisfied about his soul, but his body had wasted to 120 pounds. There were no miracle drugs. He had a skeleton-like appearance. Visitors offered encouragement, advice, remedies and prayers. The promise of healing was constantly held out to him, but it didn't happen. The Methodist pastor advised him to exercise patience—something for which he was ill-equipped, then and now.

Elmer Roberts entered his young brother's bedroom. The wall nearest the bed had only recently been repapered to hide the blood spat upon the wall from the constant hacking, hemorrhaging cough. Gently, he reached his arms under Oral's gaunt frame and carried him to the back seat of a borrowed car. "Oral, there's a preacher holding a revival in Ada and people are being healed. I'm taking you there."

As Oral relates it, while traveling to the meeting, God spoke to him: "SON, I AM GOING TO HEAL YOU AND YOU ARE TO TAKE THE MESSAGE OF MY HEALING POWER TO YOUR GENERATION!"

At the meeting, when his time to be prayed for arrived, Oral recognized immediately that this evangelist's prayers were different than any others previous. Others had begged God for intervention, for healing if it were God's will. This evangelist presumed no questions: God *wanted* to heal Oral Roberts. All that was needed was the faith to believe and to receive. Within moments of the prayer, Oral was standing to proclaim his healing.

From this point Oral's future took a radically different shape from the one he had previously envisioned. This was the end of those dreams of college, law school and politics. He would not graduate from high school. Instead, upon reaching age 26, he would take the General Educational Development test originally designed for returning World War II veterans (which Oral was not) and *score the highest mark* then on record at Phillips University in Enid. Although he would amass nearly 90 hours of college work with a *perfect grade-point average,* he would never graduate from college. Instead, he would found a University better known around the world than any of the colleges he attended. In the place of becoming a lawyer, he would found a law school. He would not be elected governor, but he would counsel with governors.

But I'm rushing my story. Shortly after his remarkable cure, Oral was ordained as a minister in the Pentecostal Holiness Church. He worked as an evangelist, teaming with his father. Later, he married Evelyn Fahnestock (my mother played piano for Mr. Fahnestock's revivals). A school teacher, Evelyn was steady and capable with both feet on the ground. She still retains a transparency that reveals a kind of basic honesty and goodness. Though she lives in luxury, you get the feeling that she could be satisfied tomorrow with much less. Her down-to-earthness was a needed requisite to the man with stars in his eyes whom she married.

After their marriage Oral took a pastorate in Shawnee, where he attended Oklahoma Baptist University. For a brief period, he pastored in Toccoa, Georgia; then he moved to Enid, Oklahoma where he pastored the local Pentecostal Holiness Church ("Evangelistic Center" was its name) and attended Phillips University. He was a guiding force in the founding of Southwestern Bible College, a Pentecostal Holiness Church college in Oklahoma City. While pursuing his own college work and managing his pastorate, he drove from Enid to Oklahoma City weekly to teach classes in religious education.

In 1947 Oral underwent a period of deep dissatisfaction. He fasted for weeks, and for thirty straight days he read the four Gospels and the Acts while kneeling. He became distressed over the difference between his ministry at the Pentecostal Holiness Church in Enid and the biblical account of the ministry of Jesus and the Apostles.

His inability to accept that disparity led to his conviction that the contradictions should be bridged, else the biblical comparison should be forsaken. Too, he was still poor, pastoring a little church, depending on the gifts of others, surrounded by a few-score-poor like he was, his mother was and his father was. He was a Pentecostal Holiness preacher, making $45 a week, living in a house he didn't own, and driving a car he couldn't afford.

Nothing was happening. No bright future was in front of him. No great possibilities loomed before him. He was destined at best to become maybe a medium-sized fish in a very, very little pond. But, deep down in his guts he knew it had to be a big fish in a big pond or no fish at all.

It was a strange week for Pastor Roberts. First, he went down to the municipal offices of the city of Enid. "Hello, I'm Reverend Oral Roberts, pastor of Evangelistic Center, and I'd like to rent the Civic Auditorium next Sunday afternoon."

The clerk looked quizzically at the tall bespectacled young man across the desk. After checking the register and obtaining the approval of her supervisor, she explained the arrangements. "It will cost $60."

"I'll bring it in next Monday."

Hesitantly, she finally agreed, filled out the forms and had him sign them. He walked out the door and headed down the street to a men's clothing store. "Hello, my name is Oral Roberts and I'm looking for a job to start next Monday."

After a brief conversation he was on the street again, confident that he would be a true Man of God or a clothing salesman starting the following Monday.

On Sunday morning he stood to explain to a puzzled congregation about the previous day's newspaper ads publicizing his Sunday afternoon service in the city auditorium.

"God told me he has raised me up to bring healing to my generation. But, there are no sick here today, none are hungry for healing, no cripples have come for prayer. No lame want to walk, no blind want to see.

"But this afternoon in the city auditorium it will be different. There will be sick and they shall be made whole, or else today will be my last day to preach at this church or any other.

"Further, God has promised me there will be at least 1,000 people present. The offering will pay for the cost of the building. Most important, He will vindicate His calling of me as an instrument of His healing power. If these things do not happen, I will know it was not God's voice I heard."

At 2:00 p.m. he entered the back door of the city auditorium. The janitor had heard of his crowd requirements. "There's at least 1,200." The cost of the building was $60; the offering was $63.03. In the middle of a fever-pitched sermon, he jumped from the stage to the floor. The crowd began to surge towards him. Reaching him first was a lady with a withered hand. When Oral grabbed it, she screamed, thrusting her hand up in the air, opening and closing it, over and over.

Pandemonium set in. Every person present who wanted healing was prayed for. At six o'clock, soaked with perspiration, Oral Roberts opened the back door again. This time, though, he stood on the bank of the big pond, ready to dive in. He was destined to be a big fish in a big pond after all. The clothing store was notified that he wasn't coming.

Oral kept his official ties with the Pentecostal Holiness Church despite the fact that many of his fellow ministers rebuked him for his methods and emphasis. They were ultraconservative; Oral was flamboyant. Their socioeconomic mentality, geared to simplicity and survival, could not accept Oral's sudden success. The Pentecostals had been ridiculed and disregarded for so long, they almost considered social unacceptability and poverty a yoke requisite for salvation. Oral's success suggested he was doing something wrong. A clique of preachers began to circulate charges against his methods and doctrinal interpretations. Occasionally, fellow ministers would refuse to participate in his crusades, though this was difficult in the face of the support he enjoyed among the lay members in their churches.

In 1952, at the General Conference of the Pentecostal Holiness Church, an attempt was made to oust Oral as a member but it failed. There was, however, sufficient opposition to reject a gift of $50,000 offered by Oral and his associate Lee Braxton toward the building of a headquarters in Memphis, Tennessee.

Through crisis after crisis Oral remained a faithful member. He tithed regularly to his church in Tulsa, and each year he sent a Christmas gift of $100 to his conference superintendent. Even though his continued success never depended on the Pentecostal Holiness Church—their income, program and influences were indeed small in comparison to his own organization's—Oral still desired their acceptance and deeply resented their ill-treatment.

In 1962 he made a major decision which served to placate his colleagues: in his crusades he began for the first time to emphasize speaking in tongues. His executive staff felt he had gone off the deep end. He spoke in tongues even in telephone conversations, and he pressured the staff to join Pentecostal churches. Al Bush told once of receiving a call from California, where Oral was spending the winter. There was a burst of tongues, followed by a query if Al (a Presbyterian) had spoken in tongues yet that day.

But the real impact was on his "partners," those millions who paid the bills, many of whom were for the first time hearing of tongues. Heretofore, Oral had never made an issue of tongues. Though he didn't hide the fact that he spoke in tongues, clearly he underplayed it because the notoriety would hinder his overall effectiveness. By not emphasizing it he had attracted thousands of mainline denominational persons, the backbone of his income and support.

But when he began to promote tongues there was confusion among his "partners" and considerable recrimination. The fatal blow came when *Life* magazine chose to do a cover story on Oral at the height of Roberts' tongues-speaking emphasis.

Though the reporters were cynical about his financial success, and questioned some of his methods in praying for the sick, the really devastating segment of the coverage was the photographs of tongue seekers. They were shown sprawled on the sawdust, faces contorted, apparently bordering on hysteria.

Just at the time Oral felt his healing ministry was achieving respectability, the *Life* story held him up to public ridicule. (I didn't know how much Oral was bothered by the article until I spent three months in the Association's archives analyzing his press coverage. Apart from his fiasco in Australia, the *Life* story caused more consternation—memos, new press guidelines, etc.—than any other.) Though it's only conjecture, it's doubtful if the article would have been nearly so negative in its impact had it not been for the excesses of Oral's tongues-speaking emphasis. For the first time ever or since, Oral responded to his press critics by having Lee Braxton write a letter of reply in *Abundant Life Magazine*. But it failed to blunt the reaction.

More than 400,000 regular contributors stopped giving. Of necessity Oral began to ease up on his emphasis on tongues. Instead of making glossolalia a confrontation factor in his crusades, he began to hold smaller, less publicized seminars in which he taught ministers and partners his insights. Books and articles on the Holy Spirit and speaking in tongues were published. Gradually the furor subsided. Key staff members who had balked at Oral's insistence that employees should belong to tongues-speaking churches were grateful that the pressure was relieved.

Meanwhile, ORU was being born. Construction started in 1961, and by 1962 a board of regents had been selected and acquisitions for the library begun. Though classes would not open until 1965, hiring a faculty and administrators, recruiting students, and developing a curriculum were immediate and herculean tasks. Oral had great difficulty finding an academic head he could work with. The first two didn't last until classes opened. Both were Pentecostals and envisioned establishing the world's finest Pentecostal university. Although Oral says now that this was never his dream, he did permit them initially to shape it in that direction. For example, the library's "Pentecostal Collection" is the most complete in the world.

When Oral and Dr. Gene Scott (his first choice as chancellor) clashed, Oral installed an old friend from Pontotoc County, Dr. R. O. Corvin. It wasn't long before he decided to make still another shift. (Part of Dr. Corvin's problem was that he had too much to do. While chancellor he was also enrolled at Oklahoma University completing his Ph.D. requirements, plus serving as General Secretary of the Pentecostal Holiness Church.) To make it easier for Dr. Corvin to step down, Oral named Dr. Corvin dean of the newly created seminary. An optimist and idealist, Dr. Corvin saw an opportunity to build the finest Pentecostal seminary in the world—in fact, the only one. Oral would say later that this also wasn't his intention.

For a replacement as academic head Oral looked outside the Pentecostal sects and chose Dr. John D. Messick. He was a long-time Methodist, but he came from a Pentecostal Holiness family. Though not a tongues-speaking practitioner himself, he did understand the phenomenon and was not opposed to it nor antagonistic to Oral's ministry. Another significant addition was Tommy Tyson, a gifted Methodist evangelist, who was widely known for his involvement in the charismatic and prayer movements. Rounding out the team was a medical man, James C. Spalding, M.D., who was something of a lay preacher as well as a tongues advocate. He, too, was a Methodist.

At the time, Oral's ministry emphasized the "whole man," body, mind and spirit. Dr. Messick was to attend to the "Mind part," Dr. Spalding the "Body part," and Tommy Tyson the "Spirit part." Together, they would compromise the "whole man" administrative team. In practice, however, the triumvirate didn't function as well as it did on paper. Dr. Messick had been president of a large state school in North Carolina, and instead of retiring, he had accepted Oral's challenge to come to ORU for five years, with the one goal of winning accreditation as soon as possible. With that thrust, Dr. Messick wasn't inclined to implement Oral's preaching theories in the field of education. So, Tommy Tyson, instead of functioning as a co-equal vice president of Spiritual life, was moved aside to be University chaplain. The third leader,

Dr. Spalding, exhibited personality patterns strongly conflicting with Oral's, and departed quickly.

Soon Dr. Messick was in control, both theoretically and in reality. Not even Oral had much to say. The emphasis of ORU was an inclusiveness—a tolerance and openness towards all denominations. This was the setting when Oral decided to join The Methodist Church for the second time.

CHAPTER 8

Why He Joined The Methodist Church

WHEN ORAL joined The Methodist Church, a radio preacher in Fort Smith, Arkansas, reported that a deal had been made whereby Oral would turn his university over to The Methodist Church in exchange for an appointment as bishop. Although this conjecture reflects an abysmal ignorance of how Methodist bishops are chosen (they are elected), it also reflects the incredulity of Oral's national audience when they learned of the change. Why in the world would Oral Roberts join The Methodist Church—and how could The Methodist Church justify accepting him?

Oral's own explanation of his action was simple: "God told me to do it." For those who can think of God in this conversational mode, that's a powerful answer. To fault it is not only to criticize a man's sense of obedience to God, but also to minimize the power of God. Oral feels that every major step he has taken has been in obedience to the command of God. His obedience in joining the Methodist Church parallels his answering God's call to the healing ministry.

Point by point, he can also elucidate where conventional wisdom opposed a certain course, but with him rationalizing is of minor importance. Patting his abdomen, he will proclaim, "Down in my gut, I knew differently. I knew God was calling me to march to a different drummer. He was saying, 'Oral, don't be like everybody else, be like Jesus'."

For Oral, the decision was God's; therefore, the appurtenant problems were God's also, and He would in due time attend to them. Oral's task was only to be a faithful and obedient instrument.

Having presented Oral's perspective, let me state that several mundane factors made the switch of churches in 1968 fortuitous.

First, his crusade ministry had peaked. Crusades were still scheduled, but he had topped out in 1958. From 1961 on his crusades were only a shadow of the original. He was fatigued. Not many people recognized the enormous drain the crusades placed on him. Forty-five minutes to an hour of preaching was followed by praying, including the laying-on-of-hands for the sick. All the while, television cameras were rolling, press photographers were flashing away, reporters were listening, and tape recorders were running—for hostile purposes, often.

By the sixth and final day, as two and three thousand

people filed before him, he was a zombie. I've seen him so weary that aides lifted his arms from one person to the next or helped to retrieve his limp hand from some desperate person who continued to cling to it and refused to let go. Glassy-eyed, he would be hustled to a car and taken to an awaiting private plane. During the entire flight he would sit silent and virtually still, casting a pall on everyone.

The crusades had become an albatross hanging on his neck. Everywhere he looked oceans of people grasped at him and variously pleaded for and demanded his prayers, his touch, his power; he was like a limp dishrag, but someone else always came along to squeeze out a little more. A sea of anguished faces confronted him in his sleep and vacant waking moments. Never to have to conduct another crusade would be a blessing—but how could his ministry proceed without crusades?

For a time he tried to shift his emphasis to seminars at ORU, but his partners would have none of it. On his television programs he tried teaching the principles behind his ministry: ratings hit the bottom.

He began to experiment with shorter crusades in different formats. The budget for advertising was reduced so that not as many people would come and there would be fewer people to pray for. The number of promotional members of the crusade staff was reduced, and efforts to organize sponsoring pastors were minimized.

To anyone who attended a crusade in the old days, the miniaturized event was a letdown. As a twelve-year old in 1949, I had listened spellbound at the edge of a packed tent as Oral mesmerized his audience with the story of Samson and Delilah. The oracle's voice crackled through the canvas cathedral like lightning, and he punctuated his sentences with thunder. As he marched round and round with his floor microphone, I followed his blazing eyes downward to behold the blinded, fallen champion of Israel, and I suffered with him. These sermons, which lasted up to two hours, shaped a receptiveness for Oral's bold and daring claims. Like a colossus, he stood astride heaps of doubt and unbelief, championing hope and faith.

In 1968, it wasn't a show anymore. It seemed that the gladiator had been tranquilized and the arena sterilized. Small crowds listened to short sermons. The prayer line was streamlined.

Two weeks after Oral joined the Boston Avenue Methodist Church in Tulsa, we were in West Palm Beach, Florida for a crusade. On the eve of the event, we were confronted by a hostile sponsoring committee of Pentecostal pastors. In angry accusation they vented their feelings about his switch. Oral listened courteously and tried to explain his position. He wasn't successful, and neither was that crusade.

Late one night following one of the services, Oral and I took a walk on the golf course next to our motel. The fronds of giant palm trees made their peculiar scraping music in the soft breeze. A burden had been lifted from Oral's shoulders. The wish had become fulfillment. "Wayne," he said, "I believe we've seen the last of the crusades. I'm not married to any method, and this one has outlived its usefulness." Now, to Pentecostal pastors, he was a pariah. He had deserted the holy cause and pitched his lot with the worldly, unconverted, nominally Christian churches.

Another reason for the change in churches possibly stems from the psychic deprivations of his early childhood. Even I as an amateur psychologist can see that much of Oral's drive and need to achieve boils up out of a deep sense of insecurity and fear of personal unacceptance. Though the pattern doesn't hold uniformly, extreme poverty can create a relentless need never to be poor again. The emotional damage to Oral's psyche has resulted in a lifetime spent constructing edifices which, once they are built, must be replaced by new structures—each time larger. Over and over again, these monuments declare, "I ain't poor no more!" The *nouveau riche* tone of the ORU campus speaks of the poor boy who made it big. The gleaming gold is a reassuring renouncement of empty pockets and an empty stomach. And when Oral took Momma Roberts to her new home in University Village, he was saying, "Momma, looky here. We ain't poor no more."

To join The Methodist Church meant joining people who weren't poor. Methodist churches were brick and mortar, not clapboard and frame. Methodist churches served as landmarks on downtown corners or luxuriated on manicured lawns in affluent suburbs; they weren't tucked away in "poor town." Methodists were lawyers and doctors, barbers and store owners, not farmers and janitors and the unemployed. To join the imposing, multimillion-dollar Boston Avenue Methodist Church, fifth largest Methodist Church in America, was to say, "Hey, world! I ain't poor no more."

But there was something deeper than these outward and material representations. Out of the ethos of poverty came a socioeconomic mentality of being a have-not in many dimensions of life. To be a Pentecostal Holiness preacher's kid (we called it "Holicostal Penniless") created a sociological schizophrenia, a defensive-fortress mentality against the world when, actually, you have to breathe, live, and die in this world because it's the only world there is—or at least the only *available* world. Pentecostal Holiness people seemed to see themselves as a remnant, an exclusive band of believers who had separated themselves from the world because of its worldly ways. Their dress, speech and customs contrasted sharply with those of mainstream society. Pentecostal Holiness people didn't smoke, drink alcohol of any kind, use profanity, wear jewelry (not even wedding rings), go to motion pictures, dance or play cards. Women didn't cut their hair, wear short sleeves or short hems, wear make-up or tint their hair. Church services built upon affirmation versus condemnation in-increased one's sensitivity to differentiation and seemed to encourage judgment-making. To be on the wrong side of the tracks was to be with God's people—poor and persecuted in this world, but enroute to glory and gold mansions in the sky.

In reaction, a great many people spend a lifetime proving to themselves and to others that they are no longer a crumb in that slice of life. For Oral, then, being accepted in The Methodist Church seemed to be a ratification of his climb out of that relegated minority which stood at odds with the events in the world.

He had long since dropped the dress codes for his employees. After 1955 employees were encouraged to tastefully use makeup, etc., instead of being required to follow "holiness" dictates. In fact, classes in good grooming were held for employees.

A short time later, Oral produced a religious motion picture. In it he saw himself as fat and cheesy. He looked around and saw employees grown fat also. An edict was sent down requiring all employees to have physicals, go on diets with timetables that had to be reached or be fired!

The reason for the fundamentalist rigidity of his Pentecostal Holiness Church was its doctrine of "entire sanctification." It was, in his mind, a great thought—it simply wasn't true and it didn't have substantive biblical warrants. Another area of his disagreement with them was the narrowness with which they interpreted speaking in tongues. For Pentecostals, speaking in tongues was *the* evidence of having received the Baptism of the Holy Ghost—it was a crowning event rather than a tool for living. The important thing to them was the initial gift; it didn't matter whether or not one ever spoke in tongues again. To Oral, tongues-speaking was a vital and vibrant resource, available each day for communion with God.

An obvious consideration in joining Methodism was the financial effect. If I believe anything, though, I believe that the potential for financial benefits that lay in joining The Methodist Church was never a deciding factor to Oral. That would have been foreign to his style. He never sat down and systematically calculated profit and loss; neither was he given to the designing of intricate plans for future action. Rather, his standard operating procedure was strictly hip-pocket: doing what he felt led to do and then following up the initial action or commitment with the necessary implementation.

He recognized that in recent years he had attracted a lot of Methodist supporters generally, and for ORU, faculty, staff and students particularly. But their presence was never appropriated as a module for building a financial profile. I doubt that he ever calculated how many more mainline people he could attract by joining The United Methodist Church. Oh, it helped financially! But, it was a gift—to be accepted graciously, and he did.

CHAPTER 9

A Technical Knockout

IN SEPTEMBER, 1966 I got my first inkling that Oral might switch to The Methodist Church. While still in seminary I agreed to do free lance coverage of a crusade in Portland, Oregon, for *Abundant Life*. During a breather some of us formed a foursome for golf. As Oral and I rolled along in the cart we shared, he asked how I liked The Methodist Church. I assured him that I was most happy in it and proceeded to explain why and how I had made the change.

While attending Southwestern Pentecostal Holiness Bible College, I had also enrolled at Oklahoma City University. After graduation from both I returned to teach in the Bible College. In January 1962, I was designated a General Evangelist in the Pentecostal Holiness Church. Soon I was traveling across the nation holding ten-day revivals, preaching at camp meetings, and at youth camps. Though outwardly successful—in one year I preached 325 times—it was a sterile and barren experience. For the first time in my life I had nothing to do but read, study, and prepare sermons. But the ideas and questions which my studying raised were not appropriate to revivals. The doctrinal framework to which I had to adhere for this kind of ministry seemed increasingly irrelevant. Each sermon became a performance of matter over mind.

In February, 1963 I cancelled a three-month slate of meetings in California and another three on the East Coast. On March 31 I joined Crown Heights Methodist Church in Oklahoma City and on June 1 was assigned a pastorate at Choctaw, a suburb of Oklahoma City. Overall, it was a beneficial experience though I felt a deep inadequacy in my theological training. I had always been extremely verbal and enjoyed public speaking. My problem now was having anything to say.

Finally, I decided to enter seminary, which would not only confront my theological and intellectual questions, but also speed the process for becoming a full-fledged Methodist minister. I already had the four years of college. Three years of seminary and two years "on trial" would meet the requirements. I decided while in seminary that I did not want to be a pastor again, although the study and seminary setting were intellectually exhilarating.

Trundling along in the golf cart I talked to Oral about it. He stared off into space and said, "I would join the Methodist Church if the bishop would give me a lifetime appointment to ORU."

The statement caught me totally off guard. Things seemed to be going well for Oral. After years of conflict, his own Pentecostal Holiness Church leaders were behind him. I couldn't imagine why he would want in The Methodist Church, and I wondered if they—*we*, I guess I should say—would want him. It sounded so incredible, I just put on a little smile that he might interpret in any of several ways.

We went on playing golf, and the next day we flew to Astoria, Washington for salmon fishing on the Columbia River, followed by dinner at the estate of one of the ORU regents. The possibility of Oral's joining The Methodist Church wasn't brought up again, and I went back to seminary, unaware that in a little more than a year I would be helping him achieve his wish.

During the Christmas holidays in 1967 (I was a full-time staff member then) Oral attended a party given by Dr. Finis Crutchfield, then pastor of the Boston Avenue Methodist Church in Tulsa. Finis suggested, half seriously, that Oral ought to be a Methodist, too.

Oral took the invitation for real. He told me about it during a crusade in Dallas several weeks later. We were on our way to a television station, and the more we talked, the more serious he became. I promised to pursue the matter with Finis when we got back to Tulsa.

Finis was more surprised than I had been at Oral's response. His invitation had been, after all, very casual and very oblique. But what had added to its import for Oral was Finis Crutchfield's prominence. Though Finis was a pastor, he was pastor of a prestigious, high-spire church, and this and other factors made him what some of us call a "near bishop." Given another quadrennial election or two, he likely would make the episcopacy. His social and theological balance made him a viable choice, and he wasn't sickeningly coy about wanting it.

To remain a *near* bishop," the aspirant must be cautious so as not to upset the flow of events that he and his supporters have charted to slide him into office. This need to maintain one's image and protect one's votes is so stultifying and even paralyzing that by the time some are elected, they've lost the vigor and vitality that originally brought them to attention. Adorned with episcopal rings and ensconced in lifetime security, they are no longer raised voices calling the church to new horizons; instead, the erstwhile firebrands have become firemen, going about dousing any flareup that threatens the system that delivered them to their "high and holy office."

As I visited in Finis' study in the fourteenth-story of Boston Avenue's steeple, I could read in his face and manner the dilemma of Near Bishop Crutchfield. His sincere commitment to people and his concern for the witness of the church were genuine; moreover, he liked Oral personally and wanted to help him. Still—he had a good chance to be elected bishop at the Jurisdictional Conference in July, only six months away. Helping to bring Oral Roberts into The Methodist Church probably would set off a furor; certainly, few influential Methodists would cheer the move. There were also theological concerns. A former university pastor, soon to be chairman of the board of trustees of Oklahoma City University, Finis was the philosophical and theological antithesis of Oral Roberts. So, while he could affirm Oral personally as a man of integrity, influence, and community contributions, he probably flinched when he thought of Oral's proclivity for tongues and faith healing. Indeed, he had forthrightly pruned out any budding tongues movement in Boston Avenue—the charismatic crowd had moved over to First Methodist, a few blocks away.

As we talked of the implications, I began to lose hope; but once we had explored the issues and started separating the important from the unimportant, I began to understand why Finis was so well respected. In the face of the hazards to his episcopal candidacy and in spite of his theological disagreements with Oral—once he learned Oral was sincerely interested—he revealed to me his prior decision: "The Methodist Church has room for Oral Roberts." From that point, he never vacillated. He remained willing to help, and he never sought to disengage himself from the presumption by many that he was a close personal friend of Oral's. (When the episcopal elections were held that summer, Finis led on the first four ballots; then his support waned and he withdrew, leaving the victory to his brother-in-law. While there were additional factors, I believe Oral was one of the issues that beat him.)

Finis laid out the procedure. Already, following my request to see him in his office, he had broached the matter with the Bishop of Oklahoma, the late W. Angie Smith, and had received a tentative go-ahead. The first step would be for Oral to join Boston Avenue. Second, there would be a transfer of ministerial orders, which would have to be approved by the Bishop, by a committee of the Annual Conference (the governing body of the state organization), and, finally, the ministerial delegates to the Conference in convention. At Finis' invitation the Bishop had agreed to come to Tulsa the following Monday to meet with Oral. The next step would be for Oral to meet with Dr. Wayne Coffin, chairman of the Conference Committee on Ministerial Qualifications.

My twenty-twenty hindsight tells me that I made a grievous error not to discern from Finis' manner how much Bishop Smith wanted, himself, to receive Oral Roberts into The Methodist Church. Having for twelve years been chairman of Methodism's General Board of Evangelism, he would have viewed bringing one of the world's best-known evangelists into The Methodist Church as a fitting valedictory. With that insight I could have prodded Oral to press for whatever ministerial status he desired; as it was, I thought he would be lucky to win acceptance on any level.

I was unable to reach Oral immediately to report, but that night at a party I located him, pulled him aside, and reported on our progress. Evidently he hadn't expected I would follow through so quickly. He was quite pleased to hear of Finis' response and the plans for meeting the Bishop on Monday.

Many times I've chastised myself for not insisting on accompanying Oral to the meeting with the Bishop and Finis, even though my being there probably wouldn't have precluded the comedy of errors that ensued. While the meeting was in progress he called me and reported that the Bishop had offered him credentials as a "local elder." "What is that, and should I take it?" he inquired.

The Methodist ministry has, it seems to me, more ranks and grades than the military. These include a local preacher, local elder, full-time supply pastor, part-time supply pastor, student supply pastor, deacon, deacon-on-trial, elder, elder-in-full connection, and elder-on-location. Each requires the fulfillment of certain educational criteria and carries explicit judicatory relationships. In Oral's Pentecostal Holiness Church it was simply mission worker, licensed minister, and ordained minister. I could appreciate Oral's confusion—but I was not aware of my own.

In seminary there were only two required Methodist courses, one on polity and another on doctrine. The former was a Mickey Mouse course which to pass required only attendance the first day and the last, or so I viewed it. In fact, I was hostile to its being required. I saw little benefit in knowing about the organizational history and present structure of Methodism. The dear old retired bishop who taught the course, a prince of a man, wouldn't have flunked anyone unless he asked to be, then it's doubtful if he would have given him lower than a "D."

Unfortunately, now though, I was Oral's resident expert on the organization and structure of Methodism. I confused "local elder" with "elder-on-location" and advised him, "That's great! Take it!"

If I had not permitted myself to react spontaneously and emotionally, I would have perceived the difference and might have advised Oral that the offer of "local elder" status for a man of his stature bordered on being insulting. "Local elder" designated a non-seminary trained man who, while serving as a supply pastor took a minimum of five years of correspondence study. Upon completion of this course, he was accepted for ordination as a "local elder," which permitted him to administer the sacraments. But he still functions as a supply pastor; is not a member of the official governing conference (Annual Conference), and has none of the acceptance that accrues to the "elder-in-full-connection." The ordination service was the same, the credentials read were the same, but the portfolio was vastly different.

On the other hand an "elder-on-location" designates a former "elder-in-full-connection" who had chosen to sever his membership with the Annual Conference, but remained fully ordained to ministry and capable of administering the sacraments and preaching, but only within the context of his relationship to the local church to which he belonged. Specifically, it means that regarding appointment, he was not subject to the authority of the bishop. And, most importantly, he could be restored to full connection with the Annual Conference by a vote of the conference.

My mind, skipping caution, leapt at the idea of Oral's not being subject to a bishop. Bishop Smith faced mandatory retirement. With the protection that I envisioned for Oral, if Bishop Smith's successor didn't like Oral— tough for the bishop!

So, Oral said yes to the Bishop and Finis. There

loomed ahead the requirement that he complete by conference time, only months away, the five-year correspondence program of sixty separate courses.

While that was in process, the news of Oral's decision began to leak out. There were a few encouraging reactions. Theologian Albert Outler felt it could be an ecumenical bridge with the burgeoning Pentecostal and charismatic elements. In my discussions with friends who were critical of my involvement in the transfer, I used as a supportive rationale theologian John Deschner's "Faith and Order" address to the World Council of Churches which dealt with ways to understand the differences between churches with an historical episcopate (bishops, patriarchs and popes) and those without such a tradition, such as Methodists and Presbyterians. He differentiated between "regular" and "irregular" ministries—*regular:* applying to those who trace their ordination back to St. Peter, the first bishop of Rome; *irregular:* applying to those since the Reformation whose ordination, though not ecclesiologically appropriate, had been validated by their fruits or success. As I appropriated the concept, Oral's "irregular ministry" had been authenticated through the fruits and gifts of his more than twenty-five years ministry.

A few days after the fateful meeting with the Bishop I was presented with a second opportunity to guide Oral away from the lesser standing. Oral informed me that Howard Greenlee, a Harvard Ph.D. and a theologian at the ORU seminary who was a Methodist and had formerly been on the faculty at Asbury Seminary, had advised him it would be a mistake for him to accept the position of "local elder." Again, out of ignorance I touted the advantage of being free from episcopal supervision. An antagonistic bishop could not touch him. Again, he accepted my recommendation, and on April 17 joined Boston Avenue Methodist Church.

I had prepared a news release along lines approved in advance by Oral, Finis, and Bishop Smith. It was released simultaneously by the Bishop's office in Oklahoma City and my office in Tulsa. I also drafted a letter in which Oral explained to his "partners" the background of his decision. Two days after I gave him the draft he flew to Hot Springs, Arkansas to visit with one of the regents. Some questions were raised there and several members of the administrative staff and I huddled in Oral's office to deal with the objections that he relayed. At midnight, after many calls back and forth between us and Oral, a final draft was approved. In a few days it was in the mail to every person on Oral's mailing list.

The contents of the letter were picked up by the news media, and people, who otherwise would probably have never heard of Oral's switch until long after the fact, began to voice protests. Bishop Smith had not anticipated the bitter reaction by many Methodists; hostile mail and phone calls besieged him. He was unprepared to handle it and he began having second thoughts. It was personally distressing for him because he was completing twenty-four years as Bishop of Oklahoma. He had led the Oklahoma Conference to a place of prominence in terms of membership and giving. Nursing centers, boys' homes, and youth camps had been built, and the Conference-owned university had become nationally recognized. Now, as his final conference approached, the Oral Roberts controversy had taken the center of the stage. Dr. Charles Simpson, his administrative assistant, called me and described the Bishop's distress. He added, "Wayne, Bishop Smith has said Oral is not to give interviews to any of the press at conference time. His specific words were, 'I'll not have my last conference made into a circus.' " Since Oral would be counting on me to handle the press anyway, I didn't worry him with the Bishop's edict.

Two days before we were to go to Oklahoma City for the conference, Oral suffered an attack of kidney stones. Kidney stones may be the Devil's own invention—besides, as I've said, Oral has a low threshold for pain. As he writhed in agony, I suffered with him; I even flinched vicariously. Still, I was struck by the irony of the situation relative to the Bishop's blackout. If Oral wasn't there, the press couldn't interview him—but, oh! I could envision the headlines. One that I doodled was: "Faith Healer Falls Ill, Can't Attend His Ordination."

Oral had everyone available start praying for him. Dr. Donald Loveless, the campus physician, examined Oral, made tests, and administered a shot to relax him and medication to facilitate the passing of the stones. As he was about to leave, he said: "Oral, I've done all I can for you as a physician, short of surgery. Now, I want to pray for you." And he did.

That night Oral passed the stones, and the following Wednesday we drove over to Oklahoma City for him to go before the Conference Committee on Ministerial Relations, which after a brief hearing, unanimously recommended his ordination as "local elder." All that day the news media, national and local, tried to get to Oral. I told them that all interviews had to be coordinated through Bishop Smith's office. They didn't like it; I didn't like it; but there was nothing else I could do.

At the ordination service held in St. Luke's Methodist Church that night, when the customary vote on each candidate's admission was taken, approval of Oral was unanimous. No minister in the standing-room-only audience cast a dissenting vote. The Bishop prohibited all photographers except one, who was instructed to take only the usual official photo of the entire class of candidates. Before laying his hands on the twenty candidates for ordination, Bishop Smith made a brief statement.

"Dr. Roberts has come here tonight as every other one of these men. He has asked for no special privileges, and I've not given him any."

After the ceremony Oral stood for two hours receiving well-wishers. He was a Methodist minister—though he was, through unfortunate circumstances, a "local elder." In the next year he was to learn painfully what that meant. To complicate things further, at the same time Oral was undergoing his transfer, the Evangelical United Brethren Church and The Methodist Church merged into the United Methodist Church, and the "Local Elder" status was dropped, effective *after* the upcoming round of Annual Conferences.

In July, Bishop Smith was replaced by Bishop Paul W. Milhouse, who came from the Evangelical United Brethren Church. For Oral his appointment was disastrous. Only two areas had been open, Oklahoma and Iowa. The only other bishop available to Oklahoma was Paul Thomas, a Methodist—but black. As the Oklahomans on the advisory committee viewed it, the assignment of a black bishop might jeopardize the already precarious financial situation of conference-owned Oklahoma City University. Bishop Thomas had excellent credentials. In contrast, they knew next to nothing about Milhouse, but he was white!

Bishop Milhouse had a difficult spot to fill. Not only was he following a bishop who had occupied the same judicatory for 24 years, he was also taking over a conference of more than 600 churches only 10 of which had been EUB. In my opinion, it made him extremely cautious. He followed the letter of the law in questionable situations. This cautiousness was demonstrated next May when Oral attended his first Annual Conference. This was also Bishop Milhouse' first Annual Conference in his new position. When the Bishop read the list of elders with special appointments (assignments other than pastorates), Oral was concerned that his name was not included. When the Bishop asked if any name had been overlooked Oral raised his hand. To Oral's embarrassment, the Bishop, though courteous, did not waver in interpreting the letter of the law—Oral was a "local elder" and not entitled to special appointment.

When Oral found me he was wiped out. I tried to make him feel better, but it was no use. "If I had known this was what it meant," he groaned, "I would never have made the switch."

Later in the conference, through the auspices of Finis Crutchfield, Oral was asked to pray at an evening meeting. This was the smallest of balms to his wounded pride. Moreover, wherever he went ministers and lay delegates thronged around him. But he was not an official delegate! Then and every year since, his conference membership has been a source of pain for him.

Where the Oklahoma Conference was unable to receive him in full fashion, The United Methodist Church was. He was asked to preach in some of the most prestigious pulpits in the nation. Other annual conferences and many national bodies sought him and received him enthusiastically.

To Oral's credit, he hasn't let his hurt diminish his effectiveness or contribution. He has emphasized openness and inclusiveness; he has stressed action instead of words; and he has never appealed to special interests nor pleaded private causes. He has been a credit to The United Methodist Church. In turn, he has benefited from the association.

CHAPTER 10

Pressure Politics In The Seminary

ON A recent Saturday morning I was awakened by the phone. It was Ben Johnson in Atlanta. Ben is the creator of the Lay Witness movement and director of the Institute of Church Renewal. A friend of his on the faculty of Emory University's Candler School of Theology was being aggressively solicited to head up a second graduate school in theology (the first was abolished) at ORU. The friend had seen only the best side of Oral Roberts and ORU. What was my opinion?

My mind flashed back to Dr. R. O. Corvin, the original dean of the first graduate school of theology. Corvin had six earned degress, Th.B., B.A., B.D., M.A., D.R.E. and Ph.D. He was Pentecostal, as Oral was, and his friendship with Oral dated to their boyhood days in Pontotoc County, Oklahoma. He was easy-going, and if he hadn't been able to please Oral, it was doubtful that Ben's friend would.

I recalled the trepidation with which I took a seat in front of Dr. Corvin's desk and told him that Oral wanted him to resign. He couldn't believe it. A few weeks earlier he and Oral had spent part of the holiday season together very happily. Interestingly, each of the men had placed a different interpretation on the warmth of that occasion. Oral had already decided to replace Corvin, and he figured that because of their friendship Corvin would be willing to step down. Corvin, on the contrary, figured his position as dean was more secure than ever.

The rupture was ostensibly related to Dr. Corvin's part in the Chilean fiasco. You will remember that our advance man, chosen by Corvin, skipped the country leaving us holding the bag, financially, organizationally and every other way. Moreover, from their conversations with Corvin, representatives of President Frei had concluded that Oral was planning to build a sister university in Santiago. The crusade bombed out, owing to the miserably poor promotion and a hostile press. Oral had caught a plane back to the United States before the crusade was over. Oral blamed all this on Corvin.

But there were other debits to Corvin on the ledger sheet. In retrospect, Oral decided he had never really wanted the seminary, but he had been pressured by Corvin to found it. The crux of the problem, however, may have been the condescending manner in which Oral felt he was treated at the seminary. Academically, the faculty was perhaps the strongest at ORU. Several held earned doctorates from prestigous schools like Harvard and Princeton; also, the seminary faculty was older and more mature, with less inclination to be intimidated or pressured. On the few occasions that Oral was invited to lecture, some of the faculty stayed away. The students, like most students, felt free to grill Oral and disagree with him. Oral interpreted their questions to indicate they were being taught material hostile to his ministry. Visitors to Dr. Corvin's classes reported to Oral about variances between the theologies of the two.

Oral had instructed me to offer Corvin a lifetime research fellowship for study of the charismatic field. He would have an office and secretary, retain his university-owned home, and enjoy a raise in salary. But he would have to resign as dean of the seminary in favor of Professor Charles Farah, a charismatic Presbyterian and church historian. Oral felt that under Dr. Corvin's leadership the seminary was too rigid and too oriented towards Pentecostal denominationalism, but with little if any appreciation of his own ministry and its unique interpretation of healing and speaking in tongues. Too, with my encouragement, Oral was reading contemporary theological thought, none of which he saw in the seminary's curriculum. To him, the seminary wasn't abreast of the times.

Dr. Corvin's response to Oral's request was strong and unequivocal. He wasn't about to resign: indeed, he threatened to fight the attempt all the way to the board of regents. Years ago I had heard Dr. Corvin described as a dreamer with the tenacity of a bulldog. He demonstrated both characteristics then.

I reported back to Oral, and his response was just as determined. It was costing $250,000 a year to maintain the seminary, and if he couldn't have a say in its administration he would simply cut off its funds. He demanded a meeting with the seminary faculty. In the interim Corvin called his faculty together and apprised them of the crisis. They pledged him one hundred percent support—even Dr. Farah, Oral's choice for successor.

Oral asked me to accompany him to the faculty meeting. I had no portfolio in either the university or the seminary, but since I had raised many of the original questions, he wanted me to press for the answers. Too, over the years, Oral had developed an extreme reluctance to engage personally in conflict. Even now, when a conflict arises, he prefers someone else to press his case. One reason is that when he gets extremely agitated, he stammers. Also, like most of us, he doesn't want to make extreme statements which he might later want to retract. But more to the point, he doesn't think quickly when there is conflict; instead, he acquiesces or gives the impression of assent. Later, perhaps the next day, after he has mulled the matter over, he develops his own position, positive and definitive. Then he's like an army tank, refusing to yield any ground and belching out the direst of consequences.

At the meeting, Oral stated his appreciation for the faculty and for Dr. Corvin. Briefly, he outlined how he had felt "led" to seek a change in leadership. In preliminary rounds, Oral is a master of indirectness and understatement. As usual, his tone here was warmly pastoral. My task was to see that nobody missed the point, despite the mode.

Dr. Corvin then made a defense of the seminary, faculty, students and curriculum. It was the unanimous conviction at the seminary, he said, that no change in administration be made. It was my turn. I proceeded to tell Dr. Corvin that obviously he had failed to perceive the import of what Oral had said—he had the choice of resigning or being fired. Even in the face of this volley, he was not overly impressed.

The meeting ended in a draw of sorts. Oral did note that his choice for dean (Farah) had not exerted much leadership in the sessions.

Subsequently, Oral sent a memo to Corvin informing him that he wanted me to give a series of lectures on contemporary theology. Oral had come to believe there was a correlation between his beliefs and those of several celebrated contemporary thinkers. We had talked about theology for hours on our travels. He was especially impressed with the existentialists, and his sermons began to speak to the importance of *this* moment—the *Now,* the irrelevance of *doctrine* to man when he is in *need* and *pain,* and the importance of relating one's beliefs to one's own experience and existence. There was never a hint of Oral's forsaking his beliefs; he had simply found a new language to express them.

While I was delivering the lectures at the seminary, the news of Oral's impending change of churches broke. Dr. Corvin tied together my lectures, Oral's joining The Methodist Church, and the effort to remove him. He had taped each of my lectures, and now he took them with him for playing to the General Board of the National Association of Evangelicals and the administrative board of the Pentecostal Holiness Church. Dr. Corvin equated the material dealt with in my lectures with Oral's beliefs. He viewed them as proof that Oral had sold out to liberalism. After all, wasn't he joining that bastion of liberalism, The Methodist Church? Then, in what he called a matter of principle, Dr. Corvin threatened to resign.

Meantime, in a series of private meetings, the faculty agreed to accept Dr. Corvin's resignation if Oral agreed to promote the associate dean, an American Baptist theologian, Dr. Howard Ervin. Oral agreed.

But Dr. Corvin did not resign quietly. His ouster became a celebrated cause. As he represented it, he had stood for the true faith and as a result had been forced out. Radio preachers picked up the scandal and began to make hay. Billy James Hargis, who had a practice of buying time for his own radio program immediately following Oral's, lambasted Oral's move three straight Sundays. A radio minister came to Tulsa, and I arranged for interviews with Corvin and everyone concerned; also, over lunch, I answered all his questions. On his program next day, he misquoted me and described me as being the engine of the Devil who was taking Oral down the primrose path of liberalism. Already, he said, I had taken "the blood of Jesus" out of the different magazines put out by the Association.

The logical culprit in all of this was me. As the temperature rose, Oral was pressured to release me. To demonstrate to the critics my commitments to his ministry, he asked me to preach in chapel. Faculty, staff and students would get the message that I was remaining on the team. Perhaps they would also see that I was no heretic.

Chaplain Tommy Tyson, a close friend, called to alert me that some of the seminarians planned to bring tape recorders to chapel. The day of the sermon (a bit late), Dr. Ervin, the dean-to-be, asked me to meet with him prior to the gathering. He had remained somewhat aloof from the controversy, but he was no stranger to conflict. Before coming to ORU, because of his charismatic stance, he had undergone several church trials. If you want to help Oral—and keep your job—he suggested, you'd better come down strong on belief-and-faith and let doubt-and-reason wait for another day.

Of all the possible forums for answering one's critics, none is easier than a pulpit. It's a one-way street with no chance for questions or pushing implications.

When I went into the chapel to preach, I saw that the house was packed and the tape recorders were out. Tommy gave me a warm introduction. Afterwards, a librarian told me it was the first chapel session in which she hadn't seen students studying during the sermon. Oral wrote me a note warmly commending it, though he later proffered that I might have polished the apple a little.

The sermon didn't end the oppostion to me, which had now become a campaign. Through Dr. Corvin's influence, a committee from the board of regents conducted a hearing and interrogated me. Afterwards, I recognized it had been a waste of time to go before them. Vep Ellis, crusade music director, and Billye Jean Morris, managing editor of *Daily Blessing* magazine, had protested my views on heaven. My response didn't satisfy them. For me, the concept of heaven was a mode of talking about the external worth of all creation; in contrast, the committee wanted me to affirm that heaven's streets were not only paved with gold—but fourteen karat yellow gold! An affirmation of the Virgin Birth wasn't acceptable; they needed it described in terms explicit enough for *Playboy* magazine. The ten members unanimously recommended that I be fired forthwith.

I didn't know how Oral might react to the report of the committee of regents, but when it came time for the full board to act, Oral affirmed me one hundred percent. He said everything I had done, including the seminary lectures, had been undertaken at his request. When they persisted in pressing for my termination, Oral reminded them that they did not have the authority to recommend my removal, because technically I was an employee of the Oral Roberts Association, not Oral Roberts University.

But most importantly he assured them of his continuing commitment to the ministry to which he had been called. Ultimately, a few members of the committee— mostly friends of Dr. Corvin's or representatives from Pentecostal denominations—resigned as regents. But the majority stayed on to enjoy what turned out to be better days than they ever dreamed possible.

That summer, with the faculty and students gone, Oral settled the seminary hassle once and for all. Income was disastrously low; at Al Bush's prodding he met with the executive committee of the board of regents, and the seminary was abolished. The seminary faculty was given the opportunity to teach in the undergraduate program in religious studies, which most of them did. Dr. Corvin moved out of his university housing. The seminary problem had been solved, but the baby was thrown out with the bath water.

As I pondered Ben Johnson's query, motion-picture clips from this saga flashed upon the screen of my memory. "Tell your friend," I said to Ben, "that he can count on two to five years that may be the most exciting of his life, along with a great deal of internal conflict, and followed maybe by a new job."

When I hung up, I could envision Dr. Corvin nodding agreement.

CHAPTER **11**

And Then Came Brother Gene . . .

A black, six-door Lincoln with heavily-tinted windows and a District of Columbia tag pulled up to the curb of the Los Angeles hotel where supporters of Oral Roberts were filing in for a partners' meeting. As they stopped and stared, a front door of the limousine opened and out jumped a swarthy, heavy-set man wearing a black suit, alligator shoes, and a white tie. The back doors opened and Oral Roberts emerged. He was quickly surrounded by half a dozen men whose attire were carbon copies of the first. They resembled opportunists who had just returned from a coup in South America. One onlooker gasped, "Omigod, the Mafia's got him!"

It wasn't the Mafia, but Gene Ewing & Associates, who had entertained Oral at their fifteen-room mansion on the beach in Santa Monica. ("Zsa Zsa used to own it.") And the car ("Me and LBJ and Connally are the only ones that have one.") was only one from a stable of black, four-door Lincolns, Buicks, and Cadillacs, plus a two-door Eldorado—black, of course.

Once, in a chance encounter, Tulsa evangelist T. L. Osborn told me, "Before Gene Ewing came along we were down to rationing pencils. Now all our bills are paid, and there's money in the bank to pay for the latest addition to our international headquarters."

Another admirer of Gene's fiscal genius is Rex Humbard, everybody's country pastor at the Cathedral of Tomorrow in Akron, Ohio. On national television, Humbard credited Gene with saving him from financial and legal disaster. One letter that Gene composed for Rex brought in an average return of $64 per copy. The Rev. Billy James Hargis and his All-American Christian University; A. A. Allen's successor, Don Stewart; these and many others have been beneficiaries of Gene's help. But Gene notes that before he helped anybody else, "I helped the king, Oral Roberts."

Gene came on the scene in late 1968, when the Roberts enterprises were beginning to feel the crunch of reaction to Oral's joining the Methodist Church. (I've described the dire circumstances already, but I want to set the stage for Gene's entrance.) Before Oral's switch, there had been a modest five to eight percent growth in income each of the preceding three years. The consensus of management was that, given careful planning and good business procedures, growth would accelerate. Then with no advance planning or participation by management in the decision, Oral joined The Methodist Church. For several months thereafter, Vice President for Finance Leon Hartz (brother of Jim Hartz of the "Today" show) sent the executive staff a weekly profile of cash flow. For three successive months there were predictions that the decline had finally bottomed out, but each month a new bottom was reached. To counteract this decrease, drastic cost-cutting measures were adopted. Money was borrowed to make the weekly payroll. Oral confided to a few of us, "I started with no staff, no offices, and no money. All I had was my Bible. And if need be, that's where I'll start again."

In August, Oral visited Rex Humbard. Rex had just purchased a television studio and had installed color cameras and tape reproduction equipment. He was slowly building a national audience for his hour-long Sunday morning television service. "Get back on TV, Oral," Rex implored. Oral liked what he saw. Back in Tulsa, he called a meeting of ORA and ORU executives. He presented some preliminary figures (grossly underestimated) of what television production would cost. To a management staff that was slashing costs, the prospect of expending hundreds of thousands of dollars for television was unthinkable. But I knew that Oral had spoken privately with selected executives before the meeting, and soon they were coming to Oral's support. Lee Braxton, the millionaire chairman of the ORU regents, observed, "Most companies make the mistake of cutting their advertising budget when sales are down. That's the very thing not to do. We've dropped our advertising right when we need it the most. Going back on TV is the only sensible thing I've heard in any of these post mortem meetings."

Privately, there was ninety percent resistance at the meeting; above board, response was almost one hundred percent in favor. Shortly afterward, Oral went to Hollywood for a luncheon meeting with Ralph Carmichael, who had recently provided new music for the radio shows. Ralph brought along his friend Dick Ross, formerly president at World Wide Pictures, the motion picture arm of the Billy Graham organization. Dick was now on his own as an independent producer and indicated an interest in producing a new series for Oral.

While Oral was exploring this costly venture, drastic cuts were being levied on established projects. The Graduate School of Theology had already been closed. Construction on University Village, the retirement center, was stopped temporarily. The building of new facilities on campus was virtually halted. "Keep one man with a hammer on the site until further notice," the resident superintendent was told. Because several hundred thousand dollars had been contributed for construction, a semblance of activity was necessary.

And then came Gene.

I had received a call from his associate, Duane Snyder, who had been a fellow student in Bible school in the fifties. When Duane told me what he was doing, and for whom, I envisioned one of the hundreds of small-tent evangelists who were traipsing around America imitating Oral. Duane requested that he and some others of the Ewing staff be given a tour of the Oral Roberts facilities "to see how you handle the mail." I agreed, we set a date, and they arrived.

There were seven of them, all in mohair suits, cashmere topcoats, and alligator shoes. They reminded me of the cartoons in which federal agents appear incognito on a stakeout all in the same black business suits. They were down to earth, friendly, and likeable with no pretense whatever. But for sure they were "country." The king's English was butchered, and their conversation was nearly all about how well things were going financially. Several staff members and I spent the day giving them a look at the Oral Roberts organization. Afterward, I was ribbed about the intentions of the visitors. None, with the exception of Duane, had finished high school, and he received his diploma through an equivalency exam. But it had been an interesting change of pace and no one anticipated any further involvement.

A few weeks later, we decided to sell the company plane; since there were to be no more tent crusades, it wasn't needed. At an executive meeting, the asking price was set at an optimistic $75,000. After the meeting, I recalled the visit of the Ewing staff. They had been impressed by the plane. It might be a real bargain for them. I called Duane, and the very next day he called back to say Gene was interested in examining the plane. A date was arranged and Bob DeWeese flew to Fort Worth to pick them up. Their first question was, "Where does Oral sit?" Promptly, Gene was installed in Oral's seat.

Because the group had expressed awe for Oral, I got him to agree to try to clinch the sale. Neither he nor I were prepared for Gene, whom he met for the first time. Instead of a humble little preacher who was being given an audience with the king of the tent evangelists, Gene's manner suggested that Oral was fortunate to meet him! Within five minutes, he expressed confidence that he could help Oral a lot.

I was incredulous—and irritated. But Oral was enjoying it all. The allotted half-hour stretched into two hours, with an impromptu luncheon in the executive kitchen.

Unfortunately for me, I had my "poor no more" glasses on. Nine years of college and university training had lifted me above my Pentecostal past, or so I thought. I couldn't conceive that anybody with an eighth-grade education, surrounded by men with even less—dressed as they were in alligator shoes and black mohair suits—could say anything worth Oral Robert's ear.

I felt that getting Oral out of the box that most Americans had him in was underway. If and when we survived the financial crunch, it would proceed. The new television series was now a crucial component. Where most of us had feared a rehash of the past, Oral had jumped at Dick Ross's suggestion to try an entertainment format complete with contemporary music, dancers ("choreographing" it was called) and guest stars. Oral had really stroked me: "If Wayne will help with my TV sermons like he has on the radio shows, I can do it." But here were these illiterates from Texas trying to tell Oral that he was doing everything wrong.

"I can help him," Gene said in an aside to me. I thought to myself, "You're the one that needs help."

Gene Ewing is, it turned out, one of the world's smartest communicators. He didn't have the technical vocabulary; he didn't know grammar or practice it; he wouldn't have known a complex sentence if he had bumped into one. He referred to non-donors as "hadn't dunnits," and premium incentive offers as "pretties." He spoke of "the hungries." One of the model letters he left for Oral ("'Let me lay this on ya to show ya what ya oughta be doin'") had seventeen misspelled words; yet Gene had the audacity to say this was one of his most successful letters ever!

Utterly flabbergasted and thoroughly disgusted, I managed to get us back to the sale of the plane. Oral promised Gene he would look over the letters and magazines he had given him; meanwhile, Gene could consider whether he wanted the plane. A January date was set for them to be flown back to Tulsa for the transfer, if it was to be made.

Meanwhile, Oral went to the Caribbean for a crusade. In his absence, I, as executive producer, worked feverishly with Dick Ross on the new television special, to be taped at NBC in Burbank. Mahalia Jackson would be the guest star, and Oral would preach on healing racial conflict. Dick had done a fantastic job, as had Ralph Carmichael, the music director. Here was the Oral Roberts of the future! Gone were the tent, the crusades, the prayer lines, the invalid tent, the whole sawdust-trail bit. The new Oral Roberts was the founder and president of an exciting university; he was a Methodist minister; he taped prime-time television specials at NBC in "downtown Burbank." He was speaking to issues that mattered and ministering to the hurts of man.

But that image was not to be nurtured. Although I suspected it not at all, Gene Ewing was about to change the main character in my drama; he was dismissing the Oral Roberts with whom I had talked Bultmann, existentialism, theology, and process philosophy; gone would be the inquiring student who had laboriously worked through Schubert Ogden's *Christ Without Myth*. (He would never read them again.) The man whom I had guided through a five-year course of study in sixty days so that he could meet the requisites for the Methodist ministry had finished my class.

In mid-January Gene Ewing came back to Tulsa bringing additional materials to demonstrate the route that he was sure Oral should take. Half a dozen of us had been summoned by Oral to hear Gene out. The visitor's opening words were a repudiation of everything I was working for:

"Oral, you've confused the people. You've gone and built a university and joined The Methodist Church. Not only that, you dropped your crusades and your television program. The people are saying, 'What's happened to Oral Roberts? Where is the man who used to want to pray for me?'"

Gene continued: "Oral, here's what you gotta do. Your ministry was built on two things, prayer and the mail. To pull yourself out of this mess, you're gonna have to return to basics. As far as the people on your mailing list are concerned, forget ORU and The Methodist Church.

Just start talking to 'em about two things: one, you want to pray for 'em, and two, you can help 'em when they write to you."

Though he was right it was for the wrong reasons. I watched in disbelief as Oral nodded assent.

At that time, I had virtually no experience in direct mail. I had written the original draft of Oral's letter announcing his joining The Methodist Church, and my letter announcing his new television series was at the moment being mailed to more than two million people. But my chief concern had been literary style, not fundraising potential. I was unwittingly hearing one of the greatest direct-mail fund-raisers of all time. Step by step, Gene set forth his remedy:

First, Oral needed to clear a time when he would go up into the Prayer Tower. He was to remain there alone—no wife, no family, no staff for three days. His meals would be brought to the door and left.

Second, he was to send a letter to the millions on the mailing list telling them that he, Oral Roberts, was going to spend this specified week in the Prayer Tower because he wanted to pray for them.

Third, the letter would state that when he went into the tower, he would take their letters and prayer requests with him. While up there, he would read their letter and write them back.

Simple. Clear. No requests for money. No involved machinery.

Then Gene paraded the materials he had prepared. First, new stationery. We were at the time using a two-color logo designed by an artist in my department. The return address was the Oral Roberts Association, Inc.

"Nobody writes to—sends money to—is interested in— this 'Oral Roberts Association,' " Gene lectured. "They are interested in Oral Roberts. They will write to him and send him money." His stationery was black print on white paper: "Oral Roberts, Tulsa, Oklahoma." Nothing more, nothing less. I thought it was terrible.

Then Gene pulled out a letter for Oral to send to his reporters. It was an emotional, repetitious request for prayer. As it was passed around the circle, I noted grammatical errors, and I passed to Al a note with the comment, "Shades of 1948!" I was soon to learn that I was close. Gene had researched our magazines dating to 1949. The language and the ideas were those on which Oral had originally built his evangelistic ministry.

Gene displayed a brochure that would be enclosed with the letter. He had resurrected a photo from *Abundant Life* showing Oral waiting to be introduced at a crusade. Bible in hand, he was looking up, smiling and expectant. Gene had created a caption: "Something good is going to happen to you." That slogan would one day become the theme song of the Oral Roberts telecasts. The same legend would appear on desk plaques. Sermons and articles would be written on this theme. And on every telecast, these would be Oral's parting words.

The real kicker: Gene presented the letter that Oral would "write" while in the Prayer Tower. It made me nauseous. It was a revival of the Blessing Pact—that granddaddy of all "Give God a dollar and He'll bless you with two" schemes. It was part of the Christian prosperity theme which had dominated an earlier period of Oral's ministry. In the two years I had been editor-in-chief, I had prohibited any mention of it in the publications. Yet, here it was, bald-faced. And it was bought.

I was to learn just how much of the Ewing package had been accepted the following week. A note came over from Oral asking to see the dummy of the next issue of *Abundant Life*. Page by page, Oral rejected my materials. In their place, he recommended stuff straight from Gene

Ewing's own magazine. It wasn't that Oral was in right field and I in left; we were in different ball parks! I realized how my predecessor must have felt, calling the Prayer Tower requesting divine intervention between Oral and him. I wasn't about to call the Prayer Tower.

I delivered my opinion of Gene Ewing's magazine. Visually, editorially and philosophically, it was sloppy, crude, illiterate and illogical. Oral acted as if he hadn't heard me. In a patient voice, he continued to speak in terms of *"We'll* put this story here," and "What would you think if *we* used this picture instead of that one?"

In frustration, I gathered up the dummy, the sermons, the stories, and the photos. I stood and said, "Oral, if you want to be editor, then you do it, but my name's not going out on that kind of crap." With a flourish, I tossed the materials into the air, and they landed with a smack on the conference table in front of him. I slammed the door and marched to my office.

My name never appeared on another printed piece used by Oral. He even deleted my name from a list of Methodists who were on his staff at the time of his change of churches. (The list appears in his autobiography, *The Call.*)

Oral personally supervised the next few issues. Today, where once there was a staff that included an editor-in-chief, managing editor, assistant editor, associate editor, and editorial assistants and feature editors, there's only Oral and one talented woman. That way, every issue is exactly as he wants it.

Gene's direct mail campaign? The Prayer Tower appeal was so successful they couldn't shoehorn all the letters into the tower. By the time for Oral to go into the tower, the rooms were overflowing and others were piling up.

The letter that Oral brought down from the tower was even more successful. Oral did a masterful rewrite, and the revised letter became the nucleus of Oral's "Seed-Faith" concept, as well as the start of *The Miracle of Seed Faith,* a book written by Yvonne Nance and Oral, and read by millions.

The yardstick of the direct mail experts is: "Letter is as letter does." The Prayer Tower event produced! It rescued the Association. In 1968, income was $6 million; one year later, it was $12.3 million. The increase couldn't be attributed to new givers won by the television programs; it was the old partners—they doubled their gifts, to $11 million. New giving amounted to only $1.3 million.

Gene Ewing had done it. He asked for nothing in return but Oral gave him the plane. No public mention was ever made of Gene Ewing—not in any letter or magazine or on any radio or television program. Oral never publicly expressed his indebtedness to Gene. But everyone involved had to marvel at the productivity of those simple concepts that sprang from his inventive mind.

CHAPTER 12

What It's Like to Work for Oral Roberts

ONE OF the prices Oral has paid for his success is a lack of close personal friends. His name is a household word; he has access to many important people; and he has the financial resources to do just about anything he wants to do. But none of these assets compares in value with having a good friend or two with whom you can share your hopes and fears, failures and victories. The nearest approximation to a close friend was his companion of 20 years, Bob DeWeese, his associate evangelist in the crusade days. Bob flew all over with him and played golf with him, but there was never any question *who* worked for *whom.*

Part of the problem that Oral experienced in making

friends was his work orientation; except when he was on the golf course, Oral never quit working. He continually pumped people for ideas and opinions, although he wasn't really receptive to their opinions unless they fit into the framework of his own understanding and preferences. Because he didn't take disagreement too well, you often felt you couldn't afford to relax and let down your defenses. He was moody. Sometimes, on overseas flights, he wouldn't say a word for four hours. His only response might be to stare at you or shake his head "yes" or "no." On mornings when he hadn't been able to sleep, or when his allergy pills were failing to work, he was unapproachable. In comparison a bear would seem like a playful kitten. After the initial fascination of watching him operate wore off, you constructed ways to avoid him, and especially to miss the longer trips.

Yet, at times Oral desperately wanted close friends—people he could trust and share confidences with. But it was so difficult for him to express his deeper needs and solicit friendship, most of his associates failed to recognize those "let's be closer" times until the occasions had passed. I realized Oral wasn't happy with his role as a loner after I "acted up" over Gene Ewing's influence on *Abundant Life* magazine.

At the time of our clash, I had only recently been promoted to vice president of communications for the Oral Roberts Association, with executive responsibility for the editorial and graphic arts department, the radio and television programs, the advertising agency, and press and public relations. Having come from the other side of the tracks, I was in tall cotton. And now I was throwing it all out the window because Oral wanted to put some material in the magazine that I found objectionable.

The morning after I walked out on Oral, I went to the office not knowing whether I still had a job or not. When

I arrived, there was a note on my desk to call Gene Ewing immediately, no matter the time. In L.A., it was six-thirty, but I called. Gene said Oral had telephoned him the night before and informed him of our hassle. Oral said he was hurt by my precipitate action. "I'm afraid I might lose him," Gene quoted him. As I understood Gene, all I needed to do was apologize, and everything would be okay. When I protested that I could not in good conscience agree with the Blessing Pact, he encouraged me to overlook it. "Let Oral put out the magazine; you work on TV."

That was an idea I hadn't even considered. The more I thought about it, the better it sounded. Though I didn't realize it then, deep down I was hoping to find a way to stay that I could live with. I talked with Sharon and Al Bush, and they thought the concept sounded workable. I decided to go for it, and I buzzed my secretary to get Oral on the phone. She said, "I just saw him go downstairs." I looked out the window and saw him getting into his car. I flew down the stairs and caught him as he was backing out. "Oral, I want to apologize for my behavior yesterday," I said. "It was inappropriate and out of place."

Instead of the warm and forgiving acceptance I expected, he said, "Let's go in and talk about it with Al." It was a talk I'll never forget. I've had clashes with friends and family, but they pale in comparison.

When we walked in, Al never knew what hit him. Minutes earlier, he had discussed some management decisions with Oral and everything seemed fine. In my assessment, Al had been Oral's most valuable resource. Like most of us on the staff, he had been raised in a Pentecostal home and had attended Bible college. He had gone on to Drake University, where he was graduated with a major in philosophy. He came to the Oral Roberts Association in 1956 and moved rapidly through the management structures. Meanwhile, he attended the University of Tulsa and took a degree in business and only lacked six hours completing his master's in business administration.

Because he had security within, Al was able to bring order and stability to the staff, and morale was good. Those who reported to Al never feared that he might give them the shaft behind their backs—important in an environment where the "Who's Closest to Oral?" game was constantly being played. Al was an exceedingly good manager of people, and had earned Oral's confidence—which was why he was executive vice president and later president.

But on this day, though I had initiated the problem, Oral delivered his soul of every frustration and every negative feeling he had about Al, me, Evelyn, his partners, and the faculty, staff, and students. At times he wept, other times he flashed his anger.

He told me I was the tightest person he had ever known—which was why I wouldn't support the Blessing Pact. He complained that the farm Sharon and I owned in Texas was more important to me than my work. My report to him on the salaries Gene paid his men was, he charged, a sneaky way to request a comparable salary. He said he knew we didn't enjoy traveling with him. While he had to go to meeting after meeting, and live alone in motels, Al and I were back home with our families taking it easy.

For the first time, I realized how desperately lonely he was, and how tasteless to him the accoutrements of power and fame had become. I refused to buy in. I had labored night and day in my assigned position; but I didn't feel obliged to be his personal valet, traveling companion, or resident shrink. Much earlier, I had concluded that the only way you could do a really viable job for him was to retain your sense of self-worth, which meant that on occasion you had to say, "No."

For more than two hours, he unburdened himself. Then he reached over and picked up Al's copper nameplate and turned it face down on the desk. His parting words were, "I wish all of you would throw these things in the waste basket."

We sat and looked at each other, stunned. A couple of months later, Oral wrote me a note of appreciation for my work on the television shows. In those two months, I had concentrated on television, giving little direction to the editorial and graphics department. Things were going smoothly, and our personal relationship was good. I felt it was a good time to resign, offering to work by contract with Dick Ross as executive producer for television.

Al related that Oral called him, saying, "Wayne's just found his place. Why is he leaving?" I never told him any more than that. A contract was drawn up under which I would continue my work with the television programs and act as a public relations consultant to the Association, but I had no intention of ever returning to the staff.

We moved to Oklahoma City and I continued my Oral Roberts relationship by serving as Executive Producer of the telecasts. Additionally, I had secured appointment as editor of the Oklahoma Methodist newspaper and began consulting work with several non-profit groups.

It wasn't long before I pulled two blunders in my new television relationship. Since I would no longer be around on a daily basis, responsibility for the World Action Singers had been transferred from me to Oral's son, Richard. But during one taping sequence after taping all day in the hot sun, with several retakes needed because of the shifting clouds, I felt the singers deserved something special for dinner. Their per diem would not allow it, but I could charge it to my own account. Richard had left earlier after finishing his solos. So, I told the singers I would meet them for dinner at the Country Fare Kitchen. An hour and a half later as we sat down to eat, in marched Richard and Patti. When he learned what had happened without his approval, he was furious and refused to sit with the rest of us. I apologized and explained that I had looked for him but he was already gone.

It was to no avail. Richard, then 20, had only gone to work for his father less than a year previously, he had been married hardly six months and was finding the new duties in television extremely demanding. He went from the cafe to his father.

That weekend we did thirteen shows though we had originally scheduled only eight. I approved payment for everyone on the basis of thirteen, including myself, though I had provided scripts for only eight. When Oral announced his intent to do one extra show each day I had delivered four more sermons, three of which he used. The other two he did on his own.

But when Richard followed through with his complaint to his father, Oral asked to see the expenditures and disagreed with my billing for the full thirteen. I flew to Hollywood and edited the balance of the shows with Dick, but the firm requisite of financial confidence required for spending Oral's money had been called into question.

At the end of a year I negotiated a new contract as a communications consultant only. During this time, Oral began to accept invitations to numerous Methodist events. I coordinated these as well as public speaking events or television appearances. All letters from pastors and church leaders were routed to me at my Oklahoma City office. I would answer the letters in Oral's name and follow up any requests for appearances. The criteria for acceptance: there had to be a guarantee of at least one thousand people present; a majority of these had to be leadership types (pastors, board members, etc.), and there had to be a free-will offering for the university. Almost without exception, the people inviting him were gracious and cooperative, even when outrageous demands were made of them. Once Oral insisted that a private jet be sent to whisk him to Minneapolis to be the headline speaker at a convention of Methodists. It would cost $2,600 which the sponsors declined. Al Bush importuned John Williams of the Williams Companies to lend their company jet, so Oral made it. I'm sure the conference leaders were glad they had been spared the alternative speaker offered them if a jet weren't provided—me.

During this time, Lord Rank of the giant Rank, Ltd. (Rank-Xerox, Rank-Technicolor, etc.) in London, became interested in Oral. Through that relationship, Oral was invited to Methodist Central Hall, Westminister, London, and eventually all thirty-nine of the television programs I had been involved in were transferred to film and shown in hundreds of homes. Later, the Rank Foundation established the "Rank Chair on the Holy Spirit" at ORU which chair Oral himself accepted, to the surprise of all of us involved.

The consulting relationship was a good one for me. I wasn't involved in the day-to-day staff squabbles and the only times I saw Oral were when I went over for our monthly conference or traveled to some event with him. Then, in August, 1971, something happened to change the relationship. At that time, Oral was deeply involved with basketball coach Ken Trickey in trying to recruit top players and to upgrade the schedule. For Oral, a national ranking in basketball was "an instrument for making a witness for Christ on the sports page." Ken had been trying to schedule a game with the Air Force Academy, near Colorado Springs. He and Oral had met one of the coaches during a tournament in Houston, and they had cultivated the relationship in the months following.

During this time Oral received an invitation from the United Methodist Board of Evangelism to speak at a conference on the Holy Spirit. The place? Colorado Springs! Oral felt the engagement might be the perfect vehicle for working on the coach. He authorized me to make a tentative acceptance, but only if the coach would be available.

The First United Methodist Church, where the conference was to be held, also invited Oral to speak at their morning worship service. It was the denomination's sixth largest church, and the pastor, Larry Lacour, was a prominent preacher. (He was one of the first Methodist ministers I had ever heard.) And we would be staying at the beautiful Broadmoor Hotel, with its excellent golf course.

Only after the coach confirmed that he would be in town and would welcome meeting with Oral did I confirm the engagement. Early on a Saturday morning, I drove out to Wiley Post Airport and joined high-roller Howard McCormick to await the arrival of his jet. It was on its way back to Oklahoma City from Tulsa, where it had picked up Oral and Coach Trickey. Howard was on his way to Las Vegas for a weekend and was flying us to Colorado as his guests. He had met Oral through Governor of Oklahoma David Hall.

When the jet soared in, we hopped aboard and headed off—Howard to Vegas, Ken to schedule a ball game, Oral to preach, and I to see that everything went smoothly— which it did not.

While we were in the air, Howard fished out a roll of bills, peeled off ten crisp C-notes, and gave them to Ken "for your sports program." I could see why the Vegas hotels and casinos rolled out the red carpet for Howard. Even after he gave Ken the thousand, his wad would still choke a horse.

Soon we were ensconced in our hotel, but instead of playing the Broadmoor course, we took Oral out to the Academy's course. After the game, Ken and Oral went to the Academy to meet with the coach. I went to an early dinner meeting with the conveners of the conference. The arrangements for Oral's appearance that night and the next morning looked great, and I reported this to Oral when he returned to the hotel.

Promptly at 7:30, we arrived at the church to find the house packed. We were told that video tape would take the service to overflow rooms. Packed houses, and especially Methodist churches, brought out Oral's best. His standard jokes ("The staff at Boston Avenue Methodist Church cancelled their Blue Cross-Blue Shield insurance when I joined") always broke down communications barriers. Walter Albritton, the organizer for this and similar conferences, later remarked that Oral was the most requested speaker within his experience.

The next morning started uneventfully. Oral had invited the Academy coach and his wife to the service and the luncheon, and he asked me to be sure they were included in the arrangements. "No problem," I assured him. The coach and his wife were personable and popular, and she was beautiful to boot. The luncheon would be at a country club near the Garden of the Gods. When I got to the church and found Dr. Lacour, I casually mentioned that Oral would have two guests for lunch. His abrupt response was, "Absolutely not! This is a private affair for the staff of the church to have an opportunity to meet with Oral Roberts. No outsiders!"

I explained who the guests were and the bind we were in. It was like talking to a brick wall. For the life of me, I couldn't understand why he was so adamant. His only concession was that Ken and I could give up our places to the coach and his wife. I knew what Oral's reaction would be to that; he didn't like to have to do all the visiting and talking, especially after having preached. What really stung me was the knowledge that if it hadn't been for the coach, Oral wouldn't be there, Lacour wouldn't have attracted widespread publicity in Colorado Springs, to say nothing of the huge offering which Oral personally solicited for the church.

After the service, which went great, people were lined up to meet Oral (many had him autograph books), and I took the coach and his wife over to meet Dr. Lacour in the hope he would relent. After the introduction, I took him aside and reiterated that Oral would very much appreciate their being included. Still he refused. I could have hit him over the head with the big Bible he was carrying!

Working for Oral, you ascertain soon that you're paid to solve problems, not to bother him with them. When Dr. Lacour proved intractable, I called the country club, identified myself as Dr. Larry Lacour, and added two places for the luncheon. Then I found Ken and his guests and graciously invited them to be Dr. Robert's guests for lunch. I took Ken aside and informed him of the "arrangements." I hoped I hadn't overplayed my hand. If Dr. Lacour wasn't bluffed out, I would have much egg on my face.

I hurried out to the club, arriving before the others. When I walked in, I bumped into the member of the club who was paying the bill. He had found me out, and he didn't think my "end around" was funny. (Evidently, he wasn't in good health, because his face was a hue between red and purple.) He made a few choice remarks, not to be repeated here. My genealogy was questionable, my manners reprehensible. He had rescinded the invitation.

I counterattacked: Dr. Roberts and Coach Trickey would arrive at any moment with their guests, and as far as I was concerned, they all had been invited. If we got to the table and there were two places short, it was the host who would look cheap. He stormed off.

In a few minutes, Oral and Coach Trickey and our two guests arrived. At the same moment, Dr. Lacour and his wife came in. When Dr. Lacour saw the coach and his wife, his face flushed. He found our host, and with amusement and some trepidation, I watched their agitated conversation. When we got to the table, there were chairs for everyone. I enjoyed my food immensely. Oral never knew of the complication or how I surmounted it.

Late that afternoon, we went to the airport and found Howard's jet waiting. On the flight, Oral asked me to come back to work. "I really need help in PR, and I need help with your cousin Carl" (Carl was then Dean of Academic Affairs). I was puzzled. Carl, who had been on the staff since 1960, was among its most loyal members. Oral had groomed him for his present post by naming him first as assistant editor of *Abundant Life Magazine*, then managing editor, followed by giving him a leave of absence and financing his studies while he finished his masters degree at Tulsa University and a Ph.D. at the University of Arkansas. (Carl never talks to others about his problems. Despite all the emotional upheaval Oral caused for him, Carl never once breathed a word about it to me, and as far as I know, anyone else. It all came straight from Oral.)

Oral wouldn't elaborate, but I surmised it might be the same problem he had experienced with Carl's predecessor, Dr. John D. Messick. Dr. Messick had barred Oral from any active administrative involvement by invoking the need for accreditation. The plot had worked as long as it appeared that ORU would be accredited, but Oral bucked when he realized that Dr. Messick wasn't going to pull it off as soon as anticipated. Dr. Messick, instead of involving the faculty and staff in the immense amount of self-study and paperwork, had attempted the task virtually unassisted. This didn't set well with the study teams that came to evaluate the process. Their candor influenced Oral to move to install Carl as Dean immediately. Accomplishing this was no easy task.

When Oral approached Dr. Messick, he found him reluctant to resign. Messick contradicted the study team's evaluation; instead, he blamed Oral. It was the onus of faith healing that was keeping the accreditation door shut, he asserted. That rankled Oral, who had about come to the end of the rope with Messick for more personal reasons. In meetings, Dr. Messick would bluntly dismiss Oral's suggestions, and on several occasions he ridiculed him to his face in front of the faculty. I remember a faculty meeting at which Oral introduced his concept of "World Action," in which ORU students would be assisted in finding career placement in strategic spots around the globe. In the middle of Oral's presentation, Dr. Messick corrected Oral for splitting an infinitive. When Oral tried to laugh it off, Dr. Messick persisted, and soon everyone realized that Oral wasn't even sure what a split infinitive was.

Oral brought the import of his "scouting" expedition before the Central Management Committee. Somebody mentioned that Dr. Messick had come to ORU with the understanding that he would stay for five academic years, and this was the start of his fourth year. "Pay him for the five, but get him out!" Oral demanded. A proposal was made that Dr. Messick be requested to resign effective at the end of the year; meanwhile, he would relinquish all authority to Carl and serve in title only. He would fulfill the remainder of his contract as a consultant. (His memberships in academic associations would be maintained.)

He acquiesced. Indicative of Oral's need to have people he fired feel good, the huge classroom, library and administration building was named the John D. Messick Learning Resources Center at an appropriate ceremony.

With Dr. Messick out of the way, at last Oral had an academic head who knew who was in charge. Or did he? Carl was willing to accord Oral his due respect; still, he recognized the precarious state at that time of the accreditation process. Dr. Messick's departure could in itself be fatal. Apart from Dr. Messick's failure to involve the faculty, he had rightly been concerned about Oral's intrusions upon the internal affairs of the academic community. Nobody on the various study teams who came on campus could abide faith healing; Oral was synonymous with the concept and they made no bones about it.

Within the context of this dilemma, Carl began working to gain accreditation for the university with the North Central Association of Colleges and Secondary Schools. But whenever conflicts arose between Oral and him, and they did, Carl always made it clear that he wanted nothing done that would endanger accreditation for the university; whereupon, Oral would back off.

Finally in May, 1971, ORU was accorded full accreditation instead of the three-year provisional status that was expected. Carl had done his job well, maybe too well. Three-year provisional status would have given him continued leverage. Now, though, a study team wouldn't be back for ten years!

At the time of our chat, in August, Oral was still elated over the accreditation, but he gave me a restricted glimpse into his feelings. "Carl has a rigidity about him," he said. "He's inflexible." This he attributed to Carl's fundamentalist Pentecostal Holiness upbringing (although Carl had joined the Boston Avenue Methodist Church the week after Oral had.) When Oral didn't volunteer any details, I assumed that it was an in-house matter of no great consequence, and I casually acknowledged that Carl could be hardheaded.

With my task being PR and "help with Carl," I returned September 1, 1971, to Tulsa with the understanding that I would be named vice president for public affairs at ORU. Once in my office, I expected Oral to authorize a memo under his name announcing my new portfolio, followed by a news release to the press. To my surprise he said he wanted to hold off for awhile: that made me extremely insecure for a time; then I learned what was behind it. Oral had devised a method for cutting Carl down to size. Instead of demoting him, he promoted every person directly under Carl to vice president and instructed them to report directly to Oral. Present for the meeting at which Oral announced the promotions were Chuck Ramsay, director of admissions; Collins Steele, director of physical plant; Bob Stamps, the new chaplain, and nine others. Except for Carl, Al, Bob Eskridge and me, all had been in middle-management posts, and now the whole bunch were to be vice presidents. Oral asked us, one by one, what specific title we wanted—including Carl. Each of us had to say the title Oral had proposed for us. It was a tawdry and unpleasant affair. After the meeting, Oral told me to send out a news release announcing the changes, including a memo announcing my arrival. The regents met the next month and in ignorance voted the new positions. According to Oral's report, the changes were pursuant to the growing responsibilities facing growing organizations. (It was an interesting meeting for another reason: Richard Roberts, who had just flunked out of ORU, was elected as a regent. And, lest Oral be charged with nepotism, he had two other former students added under the guise of needing to add young men to the board.) The eight new veeps were vice presidents in name only. No one received more portfolio; instead, Carl's was decreased. And the new vice presidents soon discovered that although Oral had emphasized that they were to report directly to him, he actually was unable and unwilling to be involved in the details of their areas. Soon, he was referring them to Carl. And because the salaries of the other four of us were from six to fourteen thousand dollars above those of the new vice presidents, Oral had all our payroll checks deposited in our personal checking accounts so the new crowd would remain unaware of the discrepancy.

Once Oral felt sure that Carl had learned his lesson, he promoted him to executive vice president of academic affairs. In 1975, Carl was again promoted, this time to provost of the university. To ensure that he was in commensurate quarters, the university-owned home in which he lived was expanded.

What's it like to work for Oral Roberts? You be the judge.

CHAPTER 13

After Oral, What—and Who?

IN THE early days of Oral's ministry, he emphasized that from among the world's billions he had been chosen by God to bring healing to his generation. This calling was not, he stressed, a feeling or intimation. In an appropriately stentorian voice, God had told him to get into his car—drive so many blocks—park—and listen. From that moment, he was to *bring healing to his generation.*

Some people, particularly non-Christians, might regard this as megalomania, but many millions of Americans can embrace it because it fits with their literalist interpretation of the Bible. If God could speak in "hey, you" fashion to Moses and Abraham and countless others, then God can also speak directly and unequivocally to people of our day. Including Oral Roberts.

Perhaps God called him, but it has taken an inordinate amount of publicity and promotion to make the public aware of his divine selection. Of course, Oral says the publicity is God's will, too—to increase his accessibility. On the subject of publicity, whenever Oral issued some vague complaint about the latest issue of one of our publications, you could bet that the real problem was there weren't enough pictures of Oral. And when a complimentary memo came, you could confidently recall that you'd used enough "Oral" pictures—often one on every other page. In contrast, Billy Graham, Oral's competitor in mass evangelism, has photo phobia. On a visit with the staff of *Decision Magazine,* I was told that the only time they heard from Graham was when they had used too many pictures of him. He had requested them to use his picture as infrequently as possible.

Oral and Graham are worlds apart in style. To preach, Graham stands behind a pulpit. After his sermon, he leaves. True, he invites the people to come forward, but there is no person-to-person contact, and certainly no "touching." That format would never have worked for Oral Roberts. He not only preached without a pulpit on most occasions, but he also met the people face to face and learned of their hurts and pains. He touched them and laid his hands upon them. In the crusade days, Oral said, "Cut off my hands and you cut off my ministry."

When Graham leaves town, there isn't the backwash of letters that Oral received. There is no on-going tie to him. His converts have to find their solace and comfort in a local church. But for Oral, the mail becomes the conduit for a continuing ministry. Write him and he'll write you back. Need a book? He'll send it to you free. There is a magazine called *Daily Blessing,* with daily devotionals; the *Abundant Life Magazine* and the Abundant Life Prayer Group, which is available by phone for prayer counseling twenty-four hours a day. There's a university for your children, a retirement village for your parents, weekly TV and radio programs and TV specials for you to tune to. Plus plaques, Bibles, mementos, records, and prayer cloths. It all comes from Oral Roberts, Tulsa, Oklahoma. There are tens of thousands of pastors of both large and small churches whose ministry doesn't reach out to their every member the way Oral's ministry is all-inclusive; neither do their members place the sort of confidence in them that Oral's followers invest in him.

And it's all one man—that is, one man plus a staff of one thousand. One man—backed by an organization with physical assets exceeding $50 million, six foreign offices, and receipts which in 1975 totaled $30 million. Oral can't afford to let the publicity flag; there has to be constant promotion. The name, the face, and the results have to be paraded over and over again. Oral Roberts, the twentieth century phenomenon. When he prays for you, it isn't your ordinary preacher—it's Oral Roberts! "God, get ready, your number one instrument in this generation is about to go to work."

Affixing his name to the university that he founded was a built-in promotional device. Virtually none of his aides favored naming it after him; their private opinions ranged from "provincial" to "egotistical." Several wanted to know why he hadn't chosen something like "Christian University" or since it was before he joined the Methodist Church "Pentecostal University"? But Oral Roberts University it was, for in his mind, God called him to see that students became extensions of his religious self-understanding. ORU, then, is an extension of Oral Roberts.

Whatever the rationale, his choice has been tremendously successful. First, it immediately identifies the school as a religious institution, and one with a tolerance for what used to be considered as the fringe elements of Christianity—namely, the charismatics with their practices of healing by faith and speaking in tongues. Whatever

Oral Roberts stood for in the minds of millions of people across the globe, the school would appropriate. Moreover, the apparent contradiction between a sawdust-trail evangelist and the founder of an ultramodern university made for instant attention from the media. The happenings at Oral Roberts University made good copy.

But, most importantly, "Oral Roberts University" assured use of his name in perpetuity, and, hopefully, a perpetuity for his ministry. During the initial building phase, he often used the quotation "Success without a successor is failure." Oral's dream is that after his death his name and ministry will continue through bright, intelligent and committed young people spreading across the globe with his ministry of healing.

Underneath Oral's expressed confidence, he fears that ORU might follow the paths of other institutions that were founded as religious institutions but are now indifferent (if not hostile) to the original purposes. To safeguard this, he has begun to stress the importance of his own family. Their role is to ensure that the memorial to his ministry does not veer from its investiture.

In the sixties, the heir would have been Oral's wife, Evelyn. In 1968, Oral, Evelyn and I were in Israel. Traveling from Tel Aviv to Samaria, we sweltered because the air conditioning in our taxi wasn't working. Jet lag and the change of diet were having their effect on me. Somehow the mystique of Israel had not included such a barren, forsaken place. In contrast, the people were a delight. Their lust for life and their cockiness were refreshing, and their sense of national purpose and destiny was inspiring.

Our Jewish guide drew his old DeSoto to the curb and announced with a flourish, "This is the well of Samaria." He opened the door for Evelyn, and then Oral and I stepped out. To go in, we would practically have to stumble over a cripple, who sat begging. His means of conveyance was a board outfitted with skate wheels. As I've said, on the road Oral never paid for anything; he bought what he wanted and left it to you to pick up the tab. I wasn't sure that giving to a beggar qualified. To be safe, I dropped in some money and followed after Oral.

"Oral!" Evelyn called.

He turned, his irritation showing.

"*Yes*, Evelyn."

"Oral, you walked right by this crippled man. Aren't you going to pray for him?"

In measured words, he answered: "No, Evelyn. I'm not going to pray for him. I'm going to the well." With that, he resumed walking.

Evelyn overtook him. "Oral Roberts! Jesus wouldn't have walked by that man. He would have prayed for him and healed him. And you should, too!"

Exasperated, Oral said in a condescending tone, "Evelyn, there were hundreds of sick people at the pool of Bethesda, but the Bible says Jesus only healed one of them. And if he had come to this well, he would probably have gotten himself a drink and gone on. Which is what I'm going to do."

Evelyn hesitated, apparently considered praying for the man herself, thought better of it, and followed Oral. But Oral's omission continued to bother her, and she mentioned it again when we were back in the taxi.

Not only does *Oral* believe he was called, Evelyn Roberts believes it. To rationalize its costs upon her marriage, perhaps she believes it even more than he does. In Samaria or New York, she doesn't back off from reminding Oral of his obligations as one specially called of God ... which may be why he sometimes seems to want to get away from her. I remember an occasion when Oral,

Al and I waited at a London hotel for a ride to the airport. We were discussing speedy transportation. Oral said, "I'd like to have an airplane with a seat for me and one for Evelyn right behind me, and the plane would go so fast I couldn't hear a word she was saying."

As I said, had Oral died in the sixties, it would have been Evelyn's task to see that ORU fulfilled its divine destiny. Fortunately, Oral continues to have surprisingly good health. When Oral turned 55 in 1974, he said that if he could have ten more years, he could accomplish his mission. His parents lived into their eighties, Oral likes to recall.

In the new framework, the heir apparent isn't Evelyn, but the third from the oldest of their four children, Richard. Momma Roberts (Oral's mother) always told Oral it would be Ronnie, the oldest boy, but Oral has apparently chosen Richard. When barely out of his teens, Richard was elected to the ORU board of regents. A year later, he was named by the ORA board of trustees as president of the Oral Roberts Association.

Though Oral has never stated his decision publicly, he began quite early to emphasize Richard's role as his successor. Pictures abound of him, singing in the crusades as early as five years of age. (Oral had him on the golf course before he was twelve; though Richard is left-handed, Oral insisted he play right-handed!)

What kind of successor will Richard be? Anytime I've been critical of Richard, I have also had to acknowledge the incredible load that Oral has always placed on him. Being the son of a man who is not only famous, but to some, infamous, is no easy task. Moreover, Oral has never been able to accept his childrens' weaknesses or failures. That kind of pressure caused a great deal of reaction from Richard by the time he was in his teens. His already average grades plummeted. On graduation from high school, he refused to attend ORU and instead enrolled at Kansas University. But after only one semester he had flunked out and returned home, at war with himself and his father. It was almost as if Richard knew what he had to do; he simply wanted it to be his decision and not his father's.

He wore several hats for awhile, but none seemed to fit. Being a student at ORU didn't work any better than at KU. Administrative assistant to the President (Oral) lasted only a short time. And he was unable even to become involved in the university musical program.

In the early fall of 1968, the World Action Singers returned from a tour of Europe and the Middle East. Richard had been scheduled to go, but backed out at the last minute. His girl friend, Patti Holcombe, did go and on the tour renewed her romantic link to Larry Dalton (now the musical conductor for the television programs).

While she was gone, Richard, though only nineteen, had decided he wanted to marry her. But when he popped the big question, she turned him down. She had seen too much of his rebellion and instability, plus she also told him she felt he was running away from the call of God on his life.

For Richard, it was a turning point. At home he spilled out his confusion to his mother and in the process committed his life to God and to helping in his father's ministry. Oral and Patti were among the first to know. Patti said yes now; their engagement was announced and by November they were married.

But what was to be his role? The answer was forthcoming. For the previous several months Ralph Carmichael had been working with Oral and the radio committee on new music. One day as we prepared to listen to Ralph's latest recommendations, Oral stopped him.

"Ralph, I want you to do me a favor."

Surprised, Ralph assured him that he would be glad to if he could.

"I've asked Richard to bring his guitar over and sing a few songs for you. But, that's not the favor."

Those of us present were as intrigued as Ralph seemed to be.

"Sure, Oral. You name it."

"Ralph, here's what I need. I think Richard has a good voice and a lot of people tell me he does. But I need someone who knows to tell me. I want you to listen to him and give me your honest opinion."

That was a difficult assignment and *favor*. It would be hard to tell the boss his son couldn't sing. Yet, as a professional musician and Christian, it would be wrong to lie about non-existent talent. Fortunately, for all concerned, Richard does have a good voice and within an hour Ralph was back upstairs enthusiastically saying so.

Within weeks Richard had signed a recording contract and his first album "My Father's Favorites" was the giveaway on the first prime time television special. He was an instant hit.

I had the opportunity to test Richard's real commitment in 1971. A major record company wanted him to sign with them. They virtually promised the moon as an incentive. There would be tours, top flight engagements, and hits. Plus, he could continue to sing on his father's show.

At Oral's direction I flew to Hollywood and met with them and had their proposed contract examined. They were utterly serious about making Richard a star. And, as I looked at their credits, the conductor and arranger they had on contract, I felt there was a real possibility.

When I returned to Tulsa, I reported to Oral on what had transpired. Oral listened intently and then said quietly, "It's Richard's decision." It was more than a week before Richard gave an answer. He was never more impressive. "Wayne, if I do that, I may as well say goodby to Dad's ministry. I've already decided: I don't want to be a star but I want to do exactly what I'm doing now."

To be sure, Richard isn't his father. But in the crucial areas of commitment and understanding they're remarkably similar. And those are the requisites for Oral's successor. Richard knows what the ministry is about and he has the commitment to stick with it.

Momma Robert's choice for Oral's successor, Ronald, also has a fascinating story. Brilliant like his father, he was an exchange student to Germany and at one time or another, has been fluent in eight languages. (In Vietnam, he taught Mandarian Chinese to the French-speaking Vietnamese!) He attended Stanford, the University of Virginia and UCLA, and at the time this was written, was completing requirements for a Ph.D. in linguistics. There is, however, a gulf between Ronnie and his father. Ronnie has undergone a deep struggle to forge his own identity apart from his father. He has an admirable inner strength. It showed in connection with his attitude toward the trust fund set up by Oral for his children.

In 1962, when Oral decided to build ORU, he divested himself of all of his personal holdings, his home, investments, everything, and put the proceeds into the endowment fund of the University. As I've related, he went on a $15,000 salary, plus the perquisites. Since this meant an enormous loss to his estate, a trust fund was set up for the children. Its source of income was the profits from the sale of his books, which is a considerable sum. For example, I ghosted *Seven Reasons Why I Know God Wants to Heal You Now* for a thousand dollars. It cost less than thirteen cents to print, yet it was sold by the trust to the Oral Roberts Association for fifty cents. The initial order of 100,000 copies netted more than $30,000 for the trust. In addition to this book our editorial department had the responsibility of preparing at least four books a year to be sold for the trust to the association. Some of them exceeded 500,000 copies in sales.

Ronnie as a member of the trust participated in the income. But when he began to stray from his father's wishes (he grew a beard and wore his hair long), Oral was furious. ORU students were sent home for less than Ronald was doing. Oral was so upset about Ronnie's grooming that when someone suggested that the children appear on one of the television specials, Oral nixed it. He didn't want America to know his son had a beard. Later when Oral learned that Ronnie was smoking and occasionally had a drink, he threatened to take him out of the trust. Usually, this kind of leverage worked. But one week during Christmas vacation, Ronnie came home and announced to his family and the family lawyers that he wanted out of the trust. That takes an unusual inner strength.

There are also the two daughters, but so far as I know Oral has never given serious consideration to them for major roles of leadership. The older, Rebecca, lives comfortably in Tulsa. She's charming and attractive, like her mother. She neither seeks close ties with her father's various activities, nor does she avoid them.

Roberta, the baby, a pleasant and intelligent young lady, as well as a validation of Oral's Indian heritage, is a graduate of ORU, where she was an excellent student. She is quiet, industrious, and easy to get along with. For a time, her husband served as Oral's special assistant, but recently began a career out from under the Roberts umbrella.

Oral's dream is that one day Ronnie will head the University and Richard the public ministry. It would be an interesting mix. Fortunately, one thing they will not have to worry about when Oral dies is finances. Like most officers of large corporations, Oral's top-level executives are heavily insured by the company. Oral himself is insured for an amount matching the corporate indebtedness. The last time I heard, the annual premium on insurance for Oral alone was a staggering sum.

Oral has worked hard to fulfill his mandate to bring healing to his generation. But healing for another generation? The answer lies with another generation, specifically, his son Richard.

CHAPTER 14

The New York Times, Henry Kissinger and Billy Graham

TOMMY TYSON served two stints as ORU chaplain. During the second round he confessed to me that he should never have come back, and I agreed. But in September, 1971 I found myself a full-time staff member once again, only this time my check came from ORU instead of the Oral Roberts Association.

As it turned out, the major task in my new position was to manage Oral's personal public relations. I had hired competent people for the routine duties of PR at ORU, which left me with less to do (for more money) than I'd ever experienced before. I had a suite of offices adjacent to those of Oral and Carl in the sixth floor penthouse of the Learning Resources Center. Before at the Association, I had been responsible for everything from television to the World Action Singers, now I had only to look after Oral's PR.

Within two weeks, I was bored stiff. In my former role, I had always been the first to arrive in the office and the last to leave, and I always went home loaded with manuscripts and proofs—and memos from Oral. Now, if I arrived early, I'd get through the little bit of paperwork before my secretary arrived, which would leave little to do the rest of the day. I lived in University housing next to Oral, which meant that I couldn't go to work late or come home early without Oral being aware of the pattern. I had to find a solution, yet it would do no good to talk with Oral—as I've said, you brought problems to Oral only when you also had their solution. (I remember the devastation of a professor who went to Oral for counseling about the problem of being homosexual. He was fired forthwith. Oral's words were, "I want to help you, and I will pray for you, but you can't stay on this faculty.")

I tried afternoons of golf at the country club (my membership was provided by the university), but I didn't feel right about it. Finally, I decided that since Oral had hired me to do PR, by golly, he would soon have PR running out his ears. Actually, it would be a challenge, because the media had long regarded Oral as they might a leper. His assessment of reporters: they were prejudiced against him before they arrived on campus, and nothing could be done or said to change that. Of course, he recognized that some reporters wrote fair stories only to have a prejudiced editor demand a rewrite. Strangely, though, Oral showed an amazing resiliency. The only article that wounded him was one in *Life*. That magazine's demise was pleasant news for Oral.

Now, from a PR perspective, things had changed. On the plus side were the accreditation of ORU, Oral's Methodist Church relationship, the new television shows, the imminent release of his autobiography, and the exciting victories of the basketball team. I was correct in my assessment. Once I primed the pump, I was swamped. ABC New York sent Steve Bell and a five-man team down for two days to do a news clip for the evening news. Tom Petit and an NBC film crew spent two weeks on campus doing a twenty-minute segment on "Chronologue." Features appeared in national newspapers and in *Time* and *Newsweek*. He made the shows of David Frost, Mike Douglas, Merv Griffin and Dinah Shore. In a single month, the clipping service to which we subscribed sent us 3,300 clippings from newspapers across the nation.

At first, Oral seemed to like the exposure and our personal relationship was at an all-time high. But then he began complaining that he was working too hard, trying to do too much, going too many places. He hinted it was my fault. I was the guy who was always arranging a special engagement and a can't-say-no interview. Somehow, I filtered out his protests. I was having a great time coming up with the best press he had ever had. Ruth, Oral's secretary, tried to warn me, and even Evelyn, but I kept humping.

With all the media, I had a standard line, "My concern is not whether you agree or disagree with Oral Roberts; my only hope is that you will be fair. Toward that end, I will provide you all the information you need." From my perspective, candor, honesty and accessibility were paying off.

Just when my most ambitious project was in the offing, Oral asked that the schedule be cleared for sixty days. Ted Fiske, religion editor of the *New York Times,* was interested in doing a story on Oral. A top newsman, Ted had an excellent grasp of religious affairs. His articles on Billy Graham had been quoted around the world. And this was the *New York Times!* It had a national and international circulation, it was mailed to almost every library, was read by presidents and diplomats, and had a large role in shaping world opinion. I couldn't say no to Ted! I determined that I would make the possibilities look so good that Oral couldn't say no either.

Much that had been written about Oral was superficial and repetitious. Ted wanted to do something different. He talked out loud about an eight-page feature in the Sunday Magazine, complete with photos. The theme: how one of the most criticized religionists of the twentieth century responded to critics and criticism. An added incentive was the possibility of a four-color portrait on the cover.

I prepared a memo and, feeling like Daniel on his way to the lion's den, called Ruth for an appointment with Oral. When I told her the reason, she laughed. She had been with Oral since his ministry started in the garage of his home in 1947. Bright, capable and personable, she always tried to be helpful to me, especially when Oral was giving me a rough time. But she also had a job to do, and one part of it was to maintain his daily schedule to suit him. When conflicts developed, she usually suffered from the fallout. Her advice to me on this occasion was, forget it! He wants his calendar clear for sixty days. However, after I read her the memo, she acknowledged that it was worth a try. When I arrived, she offered me a "last meal."

I walked into Oral's office, placed my memo in front of him, and requested that he read it all before responding. He pulled out his glasses, put them on, and crooked his neck to the right as he always did when he was bored or upset. He read the memo, pulled off his glasses, let out a big sigh. As we talked, you'd have thought we were discussing getting a squib among the patent medicine ads on the Bugtussle Babbler. Finally, he acquiesced, but his closing words were, "All right, Wayne, but you're killing me." He went back to his work, and I walked out.

I reached Ted. He would arrive on Saturday, spend four days on campus, then fly to L.A. to observe the taping at NBC, Burbank of the next TV special with guest stars Roy Clark and Skeeter Davis. While on the coast, he and a photographer would follow Oral around for candid glimpses of how he worked with people. During and after the taping, Ted would interview Oral, and then we'd come back to Tulsa for a wrap-up. I would make appointments with key leaders in the Tulsa business and religious community. On a nice social note, Ted would bring his wife.

That was Monday. Tuesday, a memo went to everyone concerned. Wednesday evening, Oral and I flew to Washington for a White House briefing by Dr. Henry Kissinger, which had been arranged by Billy Graham for selected religious leaders. Following the briefing, Oral and Graham visited together for half an hour. It was fascinating to observe them. They discussed how Graham's daughter who had married a Pentecostal was getting along. There had been some problems which Oral had been called upon to mediate. Graham mentioned trying to reach Oral after watching his Christmas special, but he had been unable to persuade either the switchboard operator or the Abundant Life Prayer Group to give him Oral's unlisted home number. Oral told of the problem he was having with his throat, and Graham related that he spent at least five minutes a day shouting, else he would get laryngitis. Graham expressed resentment at the press for their criticism of his close friendship with President Nixon. Surely he was better than some liberal, he quipped.

I knew Oral valued Graham's opinion, so I decided to get in a plug for Ted Fiske and the *New York Times.* "Dr. Graham, Ted Fiske has asked to do a story on Oral. We were concerned whether he would be fair and honest. How did he treat you?" Graham used glowing words to describe Ted. He probably overdid it, because I sensed that Oral wasn't as impressed as he should have been.

Following their visit we had lunch with Bill Bright, the leader of the Campus Crusade for Christ, which enjoyed tremendous support among conservative churches. They were opposed to speaking in tongues; in fact, their Athletes in Action, a touring basketball team of former college players, wouldn't enroll former ORU players because of ORU's identity as a charismatic institution. For the first time, Oral and Bright were sitting down together. Though cool at first, Bright warmed to Oral, and soon was quite responsive. The next year, one of ORU's graduating players made the AIA team.

Things were going my way, but my concern over one more item on our agenda kept me from feeling heady. A radio station in New York, the world's largest talk station, had bugged me for weeks to get Oral on the phone. I had promised to try it this particular afternoon since our plane didn't leave until six. Oral expressed a need to relax, so I held off mentioning the talk show. Meanwhile, we bought a paper, checked the amusement pages, and headed for the only movie that he hadn't seen—an R-rated one starring a black detective, Shaft. In the cab, I mentioned the radio show. They only wanted ten minutes, their audience was over a million, and Al Bush had said it would help the ministry in New York. The station had agreed not to use the phrase "faith healer" and had promised to screen out the nuts. Oral rolled his wad of

Juicy Fruit gum into his cheek and grunted approval. I excused myself and called the station to say I would get Oral on as soon as the movie was over.

When we came out, I phoned the station and again they assured me they were going to open with an interview, and, yes, they would screen out the nuts. I briefed Oral on the procedure, gave him the interviewer's name, and handed him the receiver.

Oral said hello and made a general response about feeling fine and honored to be on the program. Then he abruptly slammed the phone onto its cradle, wheeled around, and stormed out of the theater. I panicked. The station had assured me everything would be cordial. What had happened? I hurried out to the curb, where Oral was flagging a cab to the airport. I hoped to placate him and get him back on the phone, telling the station there had been a disconnection.

"What happened, Oral?"

"You said they would screen all the calls, Wayne. You said the guy would interview me first, then take the calls. Well, he had hardly said hello before he gave the station number and said, 'Evangelist Oral Roberts is on the line waiting to take your call.'"

I had made one omission. I hadn't explained a technicality. "Oral, they did that so they'd have a lapse of time, permitting them to screen the people and have the acceptable ones ready following your interview."

"You should have told me," he said curtly, and he crawled into the cab.

Though it's hard to believe, things went from bad to worse. When the cabbie asked, "Where to?" I answered, "National Airport." It was four o'clock and evening traffic was building, but our flight wasn't until six, so I felt safe. I pulled out our tickets and checked the flight time. Okay. A little later, feeling jumpy, I examined the tickets to make sure it was National and not Dulles. The tickets didn't say. Oh, well, we had flown into National; surely the travel agency would have called attention to a change of airports if, indeed, there was a change.

A few minutes before five, we arrived at National. I paid the driver, and we went into the designated airline's section of the terminal building. When I looked up at the board, I couldn't find our flight. The counter confirmed my worst fear: our flight was from Dulles.

Oral was as upset as I expected him to be. I felt like a one-legged man who had just lost a butt-kicking contest. There wasn't a cab in sight. When one came, a lady grabbed it. I told the driver that the fellow I was with was Oral Roberts, and he was in a hurry to get to Dulles. Would he take us? He assured us the lady's destination was on the way and we'd make Dulles in time.

We lost fifteen minutes taking the lady home, then we found ourselves creeping along in the notorious Washington rush-hour traffic. The driver blabbered incessantly, mostly asking Oral questions that he didn't want to answer. "What about devoting all your energies to getting us to the airport," I suggested.

Finally, I saw we weren't going to make it. At five-forty, I instructed the cabbie to pull off the freeway at a telephone. I called the airline and was told our flight would leave on time. (I later discovered they were delayed two hours!) Then I inquired about alternate flights. She located a flight to St. Louis with connections to Tulsa which would leave in thirty minutes—from National. I made reservations and, without waiting for confirmation, rushed back to the cab. This time we were going with the traffic, and we pulled into National with time to spare. Inside, we confronted a long Easter-weekend line at the counter.

When I handed the agent our tickets and told him

about the phone reservations, he answered, "Sorry, we're full. Your only chance is to go to the gate, get on the waiting list, and see if someone doesn't show."

I didn't tell Oral about the hitch. At the gate, the agent told me there were seven ahead of us on the waiting list. Beg, bluff, or bribe, I was going to get Oral on that flight. I invoked the names of Dr. Kissinger, Billy Graham, President Nixon, Oral, God, and that airline's manager in Tulsa. Luckily, we both got on. Even more fortunate, our seats weren't together.

When we arrived in St. Louis, I rushed ahead to check availability of seats to Tulsa. There were none. I tried every tactic I knew, and nothing worked. I importuned the waiting passengers, but none was about to give up his seat as a favor to Brother Roberts. Finally, a passenger who happened to be a former stewardess agreed to sit on the jump seat if the agent would permit it. He did. I gave Oral his ticket and sent him winging home.

Now I tried to call Sharon, who was to have met us. She was already at the airport. Finally, my page reached her (she was, by the way, nine months pregnant), and she agreed to wait for Oral. "I'll see you soon," I promised.

The earliest I could get a flight was in the wee hours of the morning. Once home, after getting a few winks of sleep, I went to the office to prepare for Ted's arrival next day. There was a note for me to come up to Oral's house. "Oh, brother," I muttered to my secretary, who was in stitches over the events of the preceding night.

Oral was eating breakfast. (Evelyn once said she had fixed him eggs and bacon and "squeezed" orange juice every morning of their married life that he was home.) As I drank my coffee, I studied Oral. He had an early-morning look—his face was unshaven, his hair still slightly damp from his shower. He was dark under the eyes from loss of sleep. On the table were the vitamin C tablets that Evelyn evangelistically proclaimed as a preventative for colds, and next to them Oral's allergy pills. (Both of us took weekly allergy shots flown in from Oral's Hawaiian physician.)

Evelyn insisted that I give a detailed account of our misadventures in Washington and St. Louis. Somehow, they now seemed less threatening, and the three of us laughed. Evelyn's relationship with Oral was an open one; she said what she felt. Her candor with Oral about his rewriting of events was refreshing. This time, however, she turned serious when she said, "Wayne, you're going to have to let up. Oral simply cannot maintain his present schedule."

"Okay," I said, my voice exuding reluctance. "All right. But one exception, the *New York Times* story." Whereupon, I proceeded to rebroadcast my tape about Ted's journalistic ability and sensitivity, about the *Time's* influence—the whole bit. Oral had been grimacing and now he spoke: "I don't need the *New York Times,* and I don't want a reporter following me around on the set at L.A." Like a publicity addict hooked on printed words, I persisted. To get me off his back, Oral offered to do a thirty-minute interview on the condition that I stay with Ted and be sure he didn't ask for more.

"But Oral, Ted Fiske isn't your average newsman. He has people begging for his coverage. He isn't going to buy into a contrived arrangement like that."

"I don't need him," Oral repeated.

I groused and pulled out the schedule I had brought along. He had been invited by Dinah Shore to play in her Celebrity Pro-Am. There were television shows, some other interviews, several special engagements. One by one, all events were cancelled except a tentative getaway-from-it-all trip to Florida, an appearance at the American Baptist Convention in Denver, and ORU's commencement exercises. For a long time, Oral had wanted to award honorary doctorates, but Carl, with the faculty's concurrence, had objected that it was presumptuous for a school with a newly accredited undergraduate program to be offering doctorates. I thought the degrees were good public relations, and at my urging Oral obtained approval from the regents. The first honorees were to be Oral's personal friend Speaker of the House of Representatives Carl Albert, who was the commencement speaker; Kathryn Kuhlman, the baccalaureate speaker (a selection strongly protested by the senior class); and Charles Blair, pastor of Calvary Temple in Denver.

On Monday, I wrote the citations. When I finished them, I wrote my own resignation, effective September 1, three and a half months away.

Oral asked me to stay on as a consultant on a free-lance basis, as I had done before. I agreed, and he told me to work out the financial terms with Al Bush.

Following commencement, instead of going to London for the taping of the television show and finishing up arrangements for a professorship endowed by the Rank Foundation in the memory of Lord Rank, I began renewing connections looking to a new career.

Tommy Tyson had been right: twice was at least one time too many to work for Oral Roberts.

CHAPTER 15

Good-By to a Unique Place

THE VERY last time I drove to my office at ORU, I seemed to be drifting back through memory and rocketing into a new and strange future, both at the same time.

Down the hill from our house, I punched the button that operated the electric gate that protected what I dubbed as "Oral Heights," behind which Oral and I lived. Sharon would be glad to be rid of the nuisance caused by the gate. She hated it. When friends came to visit us, they couldn't drive in, and this necessitated their walking up the hill to fetch us to let them in. Occasionally, we would find the gateway blocked by misguided souls who had heard God tell them to pull up stakes in Arizona, New York, California, or Alaska and pilgrimage to Oklahoma to see Brother Roberts. The guard came by every half-hour, which meant he could discourage these displaced people from camping on the lawn beside their burdened old cars and trucks. Like Okies headed for California in the old days, here they were, hoping on hope to get a glimpse of, and maybe a nod from, the Man.

Because of the kooks, Sharon did find the presence of the guards comforting, but I considered them more dangerous than the risk of intruders. I agreed with the students' characterization of them as "Deputy Dawg and his Charismatic Cops." Once the campus security chief had overreacted and done considerable damage to our Tulsa relations. Roger Wheeler, chairman of the board of Telex (IBM's antagonist), was hosting some Russian dignitaries. Their visit to Tulsa included a tour of ORU, with a Russian language professor as their guide. Only hours after their arrival on campus, the professor called me, incensed and embarrassed. While he was escorting the Russians, the campus security chief overtook the party and insisted on guarding them during the visit. To add insult to injury, the security chief refused to let them into the chapel, where Oral was speaking, on the ground they might attempt to assassinate him. Even in right-wing, Billy James Hargis' Tulsatown, it was hard to conceive of a grown man fantasizing that a visiting Russian delegation's real purpose was to assassinate Oral Roberts. For certain, I would not mourn my separation from the campus security guards.

I drove past the house of Dr. Howard Ervin, the American Baptist theologian who, you'll recall, was an interim dean of the defunct seminary, closed in the financial backlash to Oral's joining the Methodist Church. Next door was Dr. Bill Jernigan, director of the Learning Resources Center, who had lost his credentials as a Nazarene minister in a controversy over tongues speaking. In the corner house lived basketball coach Ken Trickey, who in the short span of a year and a half had won national attention for ORU. Across the street was Bob Eskridge, the ORU vice president for business affairs.

Bob would leave in a year or so to become president of a local bank.

Straight ahead was the home of Ron Smith, brought to Tulsa to build the retirement center. Upon Al Bush's promotion to president of the Oral Roberts Association, Ron had been made executive vice president. He was extremely talented and capable, but kept to himself most of the time.

Next door was Al Bush, my closest personal friend on the staff, and then the home of my cousin Carl, intelligent and hard-working, but continually on the hot seat as executive vice president of academic affairs. And here was Bob DeWeese, former associate evangelist. Extremely likeable, he represented the best of the crusade days. His confinement to a limited role nowadays was a source of dismay and frustration to him and a concern to his many friends.

Down the hill was Bob Brooks, brought by Ken Trickey from Middle Tennessee University. He had just moved from sports information director and assistant athletic director. In these roles, his zealous financial integrity was making life miserable for the coaches, so Ken persuaded Oral to promote Bob to the business office, where he eventually took Bob Eskridge's position.

Soon I reached Lewis Avenue and drove alongside the campus, a view that still surprised me. Although it was a melange of competing architectural styles—all designed by the same architect!—it was still a miracle in the best sense of the word. Ten years earlier, even Jimmy the Greek wouldn't have accepted odds that a 160-acre cow pasture would become a university with students from every state and forty foreign countries, and from thirty religious denominations.

I turned on 81st and passed the almost completed Mabee Center, home of the illustrious basketball team.

On my far right, south of the campus, and barely distinguishable, lay University Village, the retirement center Ron Smith had brought to fruition. Next to it were a couple of apartment buildings for married couples, which contained black athletes and their families. In a strongly segregated and socially stratified Tulsa, blacks lived on the far north side of town. ORU was in the far south; it was near swank Southern Hills Country Club, with its closed membership. The apartments were a necessity if black athletes were to be recruited for basketball.

Finally, nestled in the trees, was the modest headquarters of the Oral Roberts Association. Here, most of the work was done and ninety per cent of the money raised. It was an ugly duckling compared to the former quarters, the seven-story Abundant Life Building of gleaming white marble near downtown Tulsa, which, when built, had been "Dedicated Forever to the Glory of God and the Healing of the Nations." Less than ten years later it was sold to Southwestern Bell Telephone.

I turned into the ORU administrative parking lot, where some judged your status by how close you were to Oral's spot. The vice presidents' row had Carl Hamilton, then Bob Eskridge, me and five others. Each place was marked with an elevated, tombstone-like cross bearing a little sign with name and title. The lesser administrators' names were painted on the curbing. Several times daily, the security guard checked to make sure the hierarchy of wheels was maintained without insult.

For the last time, I parked in my coveted space. Entering the office, I said good morning to my secretary, a bright and attractive young lady who, after six months (bless her) still found the place a marvel. As I finished cleaning out my desk, Ruth buzzed me and said Oral wanted me to drop by the house before I left.

I said good-by and backed into the corridor, drinking

in one last view of my "shop." Theatrically, I closed the door behind me—I was, I told myself, closing a chapter of my life. Then I hurried down to my car.

Now I made the reverse journey. I tooted my horn at Sharon as I drove by our house and around the corner to Oral's. It was a beautiful home, neither modest nor ostentatious. It rested on a hill, affording a look over the treetops at Tulsa. There was a large parking lot for accommodating guests at frequent meetings and receptions. There was also a swimming pool, seldom used. A carport housed the 300SEL Mercedes Benz that Oral drove, and alongside it was the smaller 280SL Mercedes used by Evelyn. She still griped about Oral's trading off her Pontiac.

There was a large den—now incredibly dark—,with fireplace, that accommodated the receptions and prayer meetings. Time and again, I had watched the Roberts' version of musical chairs—in rotation, participants were placed in the center for special prayer. There was also a dining room, although I had never known it to be used. Off the den was an office. It was poorly heated and required two portable heating units to keep Oral's feet warm in winter time. Across the house was a small library, filled with Oral's books, several Bibles, and a large color TV.

At the back of the house were Oral's bedroom and a large walk-in bath, where Oral's carefully coiffed and thinning hair was washed and dried every morning. He maintained a large wardrobe of suits, necessitated by his television appearances. His $17\frac{1}{2}$-inch neck in combination with small shoulders and long arms made fitting difficult. When he found shirts that he liked, he sometimes bought a dozen, and once he purchased twenty pairs of slacks. Then there were the rows of Johnston Murphy shoes, and the boots which he wore mostly now—they hid his favored white golf socks with narrow red and blue circles at the top.

Evelyn's bedroom was next door. Adjacent to the bedrooms was a lounging room. Up the hall was a guest room and the rooms formerly used by Richard and Roberta.

It was a beautiful home, tastefully done. It had appeared in the budget at a cost of $75,000, although it cost double that. The difference had been taken care of in one of the numerous add-on's in the cost-plus building projects on the campus by Manhattan Construction.

Our meeting was brief. Oral volunteered to pay my moving expenses. We briefly rehearsed the arrangements underway for his induction two months later into the Oklahoma Hall of Fame and for a speaking engagement at Fort Hood, near Killeen, Texas.

Three weeks later, working now in my freelance capacity, I was in Fort Hood when a call came from Al Bush. He had resigned. "Wayne, he wants to review every reporting relationship (contracts with staff members) I have. I've written yours up and have sent it to him for approval. Since it's identical to the earlier one, I'm sure he will approve it. He will be in touch."

One week later, I called home from New York, where I had met with the publisher of a book I was collaborating on with one of the returned P.O.W.'s. Sharon told me there was a letter from Oral spelling out "the new terms." No hospitalization and a reduction of fifty dollars per month in retainer. On the flight home, I thought it over and decided this must be his way of firing me; Oral had always said his policy was to pay his top people a little more than they asked.

I wrote a note expressing appreciation for his offer. "There really isn't anything you need from me that I can provide for this amount," I concluded.

That effectively severed our professional relationship of more than ten years, which had of late deteriorated into an on-again, off-again tone. I felt a twinge of sadness—and a pang of insecurity, since this had been my major source of income since 1965.

A few months later, I talked to Ruth. She said that in the interim, a request had come from the Mike Douglas Show, and Oral had scribbled on the letter: "Have Wayne handle." She reminded him that I was no longer around. He laughed and said, "You know, I still miss Wayne."

I've seen Oral twice—once at the country club, where I was playing golf, and later when I attended a basketball game between the cross-town rivals, TU and ORU. Following the game, we had a very warm visit for about twenty minutes. He talked mostly about his recent physical problems. That winter he had been sick much of the time, and he feared his old adversary, tuberculosis, was returning. It was as if Oral, who had listened to hundreds of thousands of sick people, needed someone to listen to him.

I visited with Al Bush the other day. We talked of how it felt to be no longer associated with Oral. Al had been with him from 1956 to 1972, and a consultant until 1974. Now he was off the board of trustees of the Association and the ORU board of regents. But his response was, "Wayne, I'm glad I left, but I must confess I miss the excitement, the controversy, the whole mix that made it such a unique place."

I know what he meant. Many times now as I sit in my little office with a part-time secretary and direct my own, quiet little world, I've had those same feelings. I make it a point never to watch the television shows, read the magazines, or listen to the radio programs (I would ruin the pleasure of it with my second-guessing), yet I know without question that the man portrayed therein made an incredible impact on my life, as he has on the lives of millions of others. Sometimes I think the impact was good, other times bad. Whichever, that's the way it was. That's Oral!